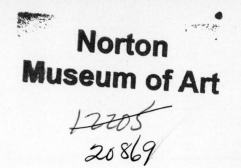
Museums Discovered

Series AN INTIMATE LOOK AT

THE HITHERTO UNPUBLISHED OR

LESSER-KNOWN ART TREASURES OF

THE SMALL MUSEUMS OF THE WORLD.

Museums Discovered

Series edited by Sir John Rothenstein

Otterlo, Holland

THE KRÖLLER-MÜLLER MUSEUM

TEXT BY

ELLEN JOOSTEN, *Assistant Director*

Shorewood Publishers, Inc.

NEW YORK

Museums Discovered | THE
KRÖLLER-MÜLLER
MUSEUM

INTRODUCTION

It is impossible to speak about the Kröller-Müller Museum simply as a sublime collection of works of art assembled by a passionate art lover, although this is the aspect it presents to those unfamiliar with its complex history.

Mrs. Kröller was motivated by another purpose than that of most collectors: the wish to create a "monument" counted heavily with her, so heavily in fact that she sought to differentiate between personal and impersonal collecting, between what she thought *beautiful* and what she thought *important*. Before 1911, when this dividing line was first drawn, Mrs. Kröller had purchased works of art, as she herself said, "from personal motives", after 1911 she collected "impersonally and purposefully," almost like a museum director who knows himself responsible to others for his purchases.

The wish to collect works of art came late and suddenly, and in this too Mrs. Kröller differed from most collectors. In fact, there is in her life before 1906 practically nothing indicative of a sensitivity to art. At the age of nineteen, in 1888, she had married the future owner of an international business concern. The family lived in a stately country house near The Hague, furnished and decorated no differently from so many others of the period. Occasionally Mrs. Kröller would add some delftware or old tiles. And then, early in 1909, she hung in this highly conventional setting three pictures by Van Gogh—the beginning of a collection that was to grow, by the time of her death thirty years later, to include some 90 paintings and 170 drawings by Van Gogh and hundreds of paintings, sculptures, and drawings by other masters.

The man who roused Mrs. Kröller's interest in—eventually passion for—art was a young and opinionated artist and art expert, H. P. Bremmer, one of the then very few who admired Van Gogh's work. Mrs. Kröller, much alone after her four children had entered high school, was one of the numerous residents of The Hague who attended Bremmer's lectures between 1906 and 1909. Stimulated by him, she started to buy, casually, drawings and paintings by Dutch contemporaries. Apparently the strongest urge behind this new interest was her wish to understand, to penetrate to the very core of culture—more especially of contemporary culture. Mrs. Kröller's intense, almost explosive reaction to Bremmer's lectures proves how unconditional her response was, once the readiness to surrender was complete.

The period from 1909 to 1911 was highly important in the lives of the Kröllers. With Bremmer as Mrs. Kröller's constant adviser, the foundations of the collection of art were laid. In Hoge Veluwe, in the east of Holland, enormous stretches of poor heath and sandy soil were bought. As Mrs. Kröller was swept along by her collecting passion, she felt a longing to let others too enjoy the beauty of her acquisitions. More important, now that her judgment of art was developing, her own conventional mansion began to irk her. The feeling of dissatisfaction was turned into purposeful activity when, returned from a trip to Florence where she had been inspired by the architecture created for the Medici, Mrs. Kröller was able to formulate in detail how the house would have to look that would do justice to her collection, and in which she herself would feel happy.

The Kröllers started looking for a building site in the environs of The Hague.

Thinking of "the only modern house in the neighborhood" (Mrs. Kröller was not aware that it had been built by the *Jugendstil* pioneer Henri van de Velde), and of another house by the Dutch architect H. P. Berlage, Mrs. Kröller traveled to Berlin to see Peter Behrens, then one of the greatest architectural authorities in Germany. The negotiations with Behrens took months, but his plans did not entirely satisfy her: the design was too austere, too compactly self-contained and symmetrical, taking no account of the character of the landscape in which it would be built but, on the contrary, in conflict with it. Then came the end of 1911, and surgery forced Mrs. Kröller to a new, concrete formulation of her wishes. For the first time she stated that the new building would have to be both a dwelling house and a museum, and that the collection would be turned over to the community after her death.

Her wavering in regard to Behrens' plans continued until Mr. Kröller helped his wife to a decision: he ordered constructed, on the chosen site, a wood and canvas model in the full size and color projected in Behrens' plans. It finally became clear that the plan did not answer Mrs. Kröller's wishes, and it was relinquished. The commission was then given to Behrens' young assistant, Mies van der Rohe. Full of a new enthusiasm, Mrs. Kröller cooperated closely with Mies during the same period of 1912 in which her art purchases reached a climax. She bought, principally in France, twenty-seven paintings by Van Gogh, most dating from his French period. She and Bremmer visited Signac, and she bought one of his pictures as well as works by Seurat, Daumier, Corot, Monticelli, Baldung Grien, and Lehmbruck. The character of the collection as a whole was not as yet clearly defined, although Van Gogh was obviously the dominating figure. In the same year Mrs. Kröller began to buy works by Redon, one of her favorites; she bought a number of Mondrian's newest works between 1913 and 1919, and added the first Monet to her collection in 1915 and the first Van Doesburg a year later.

In the meantime there was another disappointment

PORTRAIT OF MRS. KRÖLLER, 1910,
BY FLORIS VERSTER.

when the design by Mies, of which a full-size model was also constructed, proved to be unsatisfactory. The plans themselves, transparent and highly harmonious, make it clear how high the demands of the Kröllers and Bremmer were, considering that this project too had to yield to the power of their dream.

In 1913 Mrs. Kröller moved part of her collection to a separate building that was accessible to interested members of the public. In the same year Berlage, the fiercely controversial pioneer of constructivist architecture in Holland, entered the employ of Wm. Müller & Co., Mr. Kröller's firm, on condition that, during the term of his contract, he would build exclusively for the firm and for Mr. and Mrs. Kröller. Berlage had just returned from a trip to America, where he had been particularly impressed by the work of the architects Louis Sullivan and Frank Lloyd Wright.

Berlage's first projects for the Kröllers were a model farm for their eldest son in northern Holland, and the Holland House in London. The next commission was a hunting lodge on Hoge Veluwe, the still partially unspoiled heath region in Dutch Guelders. Following Mrs. Kröller's request, the lodge was built as an expression of the legend of St. Hubert, which is concerned with the symbolical meaning of the antlers (nature) and the cross (spirit): the ground plan has the structure of a pair of stag's antlers while a 100-foot tower represents the cross; every detail of the structure represents some aspect of the legend.

As early as 1915 it had been decided that "not in the west of Holland but on the grounds of the Hoge Veluwe in Guelders the new museum was to be built," quite independent of the Kröllers' private house near The Hague. Undoubtedly their frequent stays at the hunting lodge on Hoge Veluwe, and perhaps World War I as well, contributed to this decision. Outsiders reacted with shock. Was not the community idea, the founding of a public museum, a hollow phrase after all? Did not the building of the museum in a practically inaccessible moorland reserve prove irrefutably that in reality the Kröllers wanted to keep the collection for themselves? According to this new resolve, Berlage's plans, worked on from 1917 to 1919, were intended for a site at the foot of a row of hills, covered with old trees and overlooking the Wildbaan—an extensive, almost bare, sandy stretch. Time has proved the change of location wise; for many years the museum has been among the most frequented in the Netherlands.

In any case Berlage, possibly because of the conflict between his and Mrs. Kröller's ideals of form and art, as well as the strain involved in the creation of the hunting lodge, a masterpiece of metaphorical architecture, unexpectedly terminated his contract with the Kröllers in 1919.

All Mrs. Kröller's hopes for a new relationship between art and architecture became centered on the Dutch painter Bart van der Leck who, like Berlage, was officially engaged to work exclusively for Mr. and Mrs. Kröller and the family firm. In the period from 1916 to 1919, Mrs. Kröller bought four first-class works by the two artists who were the purest representatives of *Jugendstil* in Holland: Jan Toorop, who had introduced divisionism to Holland, and Johannes Thorn Prikker. By 1920 Mrs. Kröller, probably stimulated by Henri van de Velde, had become intensely fascinated by cubism, and bought within two years about thirty paintings and five sculptures by Maria Blanchard, Gris, Braque, Picasso, Metzinger, Severini, Valmier, and Csàky, mostly at Léonce Rosenberg's in Paris. All this, together with the acquisition in 1920 of another twenty-seven paintings by Van Gogh, largely from his Dutch period, resulted in giving the collection a clearly defined character. The Van Gogh collection was central; it was chronologically introduced by a modest group of seventy-six works, dating from the fifteenth through the eighteenth centuries, and by a large collection of nineteenth-century works; it was followed by works representing divisionism, symbolism, *Jugendstil,* and cubism, ending with a large number of works by Mondrian and Van der Leck.

In 1920 Mrs. Kröller, remembering Henri van de Velde's work on a museum and home for a German art collector, invited him from Switzerland. Van de Velde became manager of the building office of Mr. Kröller's firm and, after a short period of work on a new home for the Kröllers near The Hague, turned to plans for the museum. During the six years that followed, he produced more than a thousand drawings for a majestic building. As in Berlage's plans, the museum was to center around the Van Gogh collection. Aside from rooms and halls devoted to showing works of art, Van de Velde—intending the building not only as a museum, but also as a meeting place for persons prominent in the arts and humanities—planned an auditorium, a library, and rooms for guests.

Van de Velde's plans show a decided shift of emphasis from Berlage's; whereas Berlage's building would have been a summer palace rich in works of art, Van de Velde's was, as Mrs. Kröller had dreamt it, "a monu-

THE SCULPTURE HALL AT THE KRÖLLER-MÜLLER MUSEUM.

ment of the architecture and art of her time created by order of an important merchant family." The plans reveal a compact sandstone building of two stories, surrounded by large terraces.

Mrs. Kröller, with enraptured approval of Van de Velde's plans, ordered the start of construction. In February 1921, a railroad was built to transport Maulbrunner sandstone 1,100 yards to the building site.

And then suddenly, in 1922, all these plans seemed to be destroyed in the quickly spreading world economic crisis, which endangered the very existence of Mr. Kröller's firm. Although the Kröllers were forced to curtail construction, as well as purchases of art, Van

de Velde continued to work on plans for the museum and the surrounding grounds. His influence was also felt in the few purchases that were made during this period: Seurat's *Chahut,* Léger's *Soldiers Playing at Cards,* and a number of sculptures by Maillol. But in 1926, Van de Velde returned to Belgium, his native country, to accept another position.

In order to make further activity possible, the Kröllers created the Kröller-Müller Foundation and transferred to it their entire art collection, stipulating that the collection was to be on public view. In 1935 the land too was turned over to a foundation, Het Nationale Park de Hoge Veluwe. In the same year the Kröller-

Müller Foundation gave the art collection to the Netherlands on condition that the government would build, within three years and according to Van de Velde's plans, a museum to house it. Van de Velde revised his plans so that a temporary museum could be built in keeping with existing economic conditions, and construction was begun in May, 1937. It was decided that another site would better suit the low structure than the spot at the foot of a row of hills selected when the plans called for a monumental design of two stories. The building was moved further into a more cultivated part of the park bordered by narrow lawns, where it comes as a surprise to the visitor following a curve in the road.

The Kröller-Müller Museum was officially opened on July 13, 1938, with Mrs. Kröller as honorary director. The center of the temporary building was devoted to the Van Gogh collection, exhibited around an inner court. Six galleries at the front of the building held works of art produced before Van Gogh, while six galleries at the back included works dating from after 1890. Ceiling fixtures above opalescent glass provided illumination, the absence of windows permitting undisturbed concentration on the collection. The power of the building resulted from the rhythmic succession of galleries, each built to moderate proportions.

During the difficult years that preceded the museum's opening, Mrs. Kröller had been occupied in organizing a traveling exhibit comprising the Kröller-Müller Van Gogh collection together with works lent by the artist's nephew, V. W. van Gogh, and by many American collectors. The interest shown by the public, especially at New York's Museum of Modern Art, was overwhelming, as it had been when the collection had traveled to Switzerland and Belgium in 1927 and to Germany in 1928-29.

Mrs. Kröller died in 1939, at the age of seventy; Mr. Kröller was to follow her two years later. In the meantime World War II had begun, and the major part of the art collection was moved to the underground shelter in the museum park. During the war the outer walls of a new wing, with a sculpture hall and auditorium, were added to the temporary structure.

In 1947 Dr. A. M. Hammacher was appointed director of the museum. Under his guidance the museum acquired a number of paintings that fit well into Mrs. Kröller's collection; the new works included several by Van Gogh and others by Gauguin, Meyer de Haan, and Signac. The emphasis in new purchases, however, shifted to sculpture in the hope that the quality of the sculpture collection could be raised to that of the paintings. The museum also acquired sculptors' drawings—independent works rather than preliminary studies for sculpture.

The sculpture added to the museum harmonized with the works Mrs. Kröller had collected, showing the same preference for cubist, abstract, and extra-European works. Similarly, Mrs. Kröller's practice of including works by secondary figures as well as by masters of each generation has been followed by succeeding administrations, preserving the museum from the modish hunt for big names.

As the collection of sculpture grew, it became obvious that the sculpture hall included in Van de Velde's original plans would have to be built. In 1953, just prior to the celebration of the centenary of Van Gogh's birth, ninety-year-old Van de Velde himself returned to Otterlo to supervise construction. The sculpture hall, much larger than the other galleries, includes two fourteen-foot-high windows, relieving the walled-in privacy of the original building, and providing an exciting relationship between the sculpture and the surrounding scenery. At the time of its opening, the hall contained sculpture by Lehmbruck, Barbara Hepworth, Zadkine, Rodin, Maillol, and Csàky, to which were eventually added works by Gonzalez, Mascherini, Marini, Pevsner, Mario Negri, and others.

Mrs. Kröller had placed several sculptures in the park surrounding the museum, and the effectiveness of this setting led Dr. Hammacher to plan what would constitute the first park in Europe created especially as a setting for sculpture. Van de Velde was again consulted during preliminary planning, but he died in 1957, four years before the completion of the park. Following the plans of J. T. P. Bijhouwer, a stretch of woodland—accessible only through the museum—was

A CORNER OF THE SCULPTURE PARK AT THE KRÖLLER-MÜLLER MUSEUM.

cleared and five large lawns were planted. The expanse of the park is relieved by shrubbery, trees, and a hilly tract dominated by Henry Moore's *Reclining Figure.*

At the time of the twenty-fifth anniversary of the Kröller-Müller Museum, Dr. Hammacher was succeeded by R. W. D. Oxenaar as director of the museum. Present plans call for further expansion of the sculpture park. Henry Moore's group, *Three Upright Motives,* was unveiled in April 1965. Another recent addition is a pavilion for small sculpture, designed by Gerrit Rietveld—financed by a group of Dutch architects as a memorial to Rietveld. A tea pavilion designed by P. Elling is planned for the future.

Mrs. Kröller's desire for serenity, which she held in common with such artists as Van Gogh, Seurat, and Van de Velde, was doubtless related to the tensions that pervaded much of her life and was manifested in her collecting, notably the exclusion of expressionistic works. This motivation may decrease in force now that the continued existence of the collection is assured and less dependent on the creative will and energy of a single person. But, although the Kröller-Müller Museum may become more open to other facets of the artistic experience, the character of the museum building and the sculpture park makes it clear that only in conjunction with confinement can freedom be forcibly effective.

[All quotations and factual information about Mr. and Mrs. Kröller are taken from S. van Deventer, Kröller-Müller, de geschiedenis van een cultureel levenswerk ("Kröller-Müller, the History of a Cultural Lifework"), Haarlem, 1956; also German edition, Cologne, Dumont Schauberg, 1958.]

List of Illustrations

PAINTINGS

DRAWINGS

ANONYMOUS: FRENCH

Madonna with Child—ca. 1490

Tempera on oakwood, 31 x 20.5 cm.

Some art historians relate this small panel to those of the Master of Moulins, in which a similar Madonna is found. They believe, however, that this panel may have been painted by a pupil of the Master because of the Italian influence seen in the Christ Child and because of the stylistic difference between the somewhat convulsive mobility of the Child and the sublimated, perfectly controlled tranquility of the Mother.

Apart from the balanced contrast between the deep red of the Madonna's gown and the green of the background, one is struck by the interplay of the leaf motif in the background and the folds of the Madonna's gown. The play of the folds in the left corner, creating a connection between the figure and the background, brings about a unity. Although the Madonna is prominent, this connecting element prevents her total detachment from the ornamentation. This in turn adds to the value of the ornamentation: the flowers and the leaves acquire, notwithstanding their stylization, a directness that joins them—pictorially and emotionally—to the figures in the foreground.

ANONYMOUS: FLEMISH (?)

Still Life in a Cabinet—1538

Oil on oakwood, 44 x 44 cm.

This still life, probably one of the earliest painted in the Southern Netherlands but acquired as late as 1951, confronts the art historian with many problems: it seems to be a *trompe l'oeil*, a deception, intended to give to a cabinet door the illusion of being a pair of shelves laden with objects. The objects themselves are full of mystery: are the half-burnt candle and the gnawing mouse symbols of Vanity, and is the apple a symbol of human frailty? or is the whole no more than a realistic representation?

The two slips of paper with deceivingly precisely imitated characters cannot help us here: only the date—1538—is decipherable. But however this may be, and whoever may have been the painter (the suggested attribution to Van Reymerswaele would seem indefensible, notwithstanding the capricious accumulation in the upper right-hand corner), this little panel is one of the most imposing items in the collection of ancient art by virtue of the mellow light, the great sensitivity of the colors, and the clear but never rigid division of the plane. The succession of leather, glass, and wooden objects (the wooden objects are hunting cups screwed one inside the other) is opposed to the suspended inkpot and book strap and the oblique objects that interrupt the vertical rhythm. In this way the painter reaches a marvelous harmony between the austere and transparent basic scheme of horizontal and vertical, and an occasionally manneristic mobility characteristic of a great part of the painting of his time and environment.

BRUYN, BARTHEL THE ELDER

b. Wesel (?), 1492/3–d. Keulen, 1555

Portrait of Jane-Loyse Tissier—1524

Oil on panel, 61 x 51 cm.

This portrait of Jane-Loyse Tissier is the right leaf of a diptych; on the left leaf, which is in Vienna Kunsthistorisches Museum, her husband is portrayed. A "Vanity" still life is on the back of the panel: Barthel Bruyn and his contemporaries repeatedly depicted symbols of transiency on the backs of their portraits.

The carnation in Jane Tissier's hand appears in many portraits of bridal couples in this period. The bride customarily offered the flower to the man during the marriage ceremony, probably as a charm against evil spirits.

Although Bruyn lived in Cologne the greater part of his life, he shows in his work an affinity to the painters of the Northern Netherlands. This portrait is a manifestation of Bruyn's great skill as a craftsman. The firm, clearly outlined forms, the warm, contrasting colors, and the delicate sensitivity with which he modeled the face prove that he painted this portrait after having reached a mature mastery of his art.

BALDUNG GRIEN, HANS

b. Schwäbisch-Gemund, 1484/5–
d. Strasbourg, 1545

Venus and Amor—1524-25

Oil on limewood, 208.3 x 84 cm.

In 1525 Baldung Grien painted a series of four monumental nude figures: Adam, Eve, Judith with the head of Holofernes, and this Venus. Professor Carl Koch, the Baldung expert, wonders whether these might be part of a still larger series, portraying prototypes of human weakness and heroism. Mrs. Kröller, notwithstanding the limitations which she observed in regard to ancient art, chose this panel to represent the period in which the medieval vision changed into the Renaissance vision.

Because of the plaster-like color of the body, the effect of the figure is compelling and monumental. The coquettish torsion of the upper part of the body and the ornamental undulation of the hair are contrasted, with perfect control, to the head on the full column of the neck and the sturdy hips. The dwarfish little figure of Cupid, with his almost hooflike foot, strongly stresses the royal attitude of Venus. The partly lifted bandage before the eyes of the little boy might indicate that he wants to free himself from his blind infatuation—his sinful love. The form on which Cupid sits is probably a symbol of the world, which was depicted as an egg-shaped ball at the time this picture was executed.

CRANACH, LUCAS THE ELDER

b. Kronach, 1472–d. Weimar, 1553

Venus with Amor as a Honey-Thief—
after 1537

Oil on limewood, 174 x 66.5 cm.

A favorite anecdote of the Humanists, taken from the *Idylls* of Theocritus, concerns Cupid and Venus. The latter tells Cupid, who has been stung by bees, "The arrows you shoot at human beings are really no less painful than the sting of the bee about which you are complaining."

The dating of this painting is derived from the studio mark —the dragon with the flattened bird's wings—which does not appear until after 1537. In that year the Elector of Saxony appointed Cranach, whose Wittenberg studio was highly respected, Mayor of that Humanist town.

The female type portrayed here as Venus is repeatedly found in Cranach's work: the mixture of sensual allure and elegant sophistication, which almost leads to a perverse coquetry, is characteristic of the majority of his nude figures. Cranach's Venus is less royal, if perhaps more delicate of nuance, than the one by Baldung Grien, and the relationship between Venus and Cupid is more concrete and human. Although the figure is less plastic in execution than Baldung's, the melodious flow of the long contours and the subtle mastery of painterly technique, particularly apparent in the veil, are truly entrancing.

SCHOOTEN, FLORIS VAN

b. (?)—d. Haarlem, 1655 (?)

Breakfast—ca. 1615-20

Oil on oakwood, 47 x 84 cm.

In the Netherlands, at the beginning of the seventeenth century, still lifes were classified into distinct categories. One of the fixed themes was the so-called "little banquet," in which the details of a meal were depicted.

Floris van Schooten belonged to the group of artists who made an important contribution to the development of still life. In this rather early work the viewpoint is high and the objects are carefully grouped in rows, so that intersections are strictly avoided. Symmetrically arranged diagonals enliven the firmly horizontal composition.

Because of the objective precision with which all objects are rendered, and the harmonious disposition of light and dark and cool and warm colors, the painting has acquired a great convincing power. Van Schooten was not very sensitive to the effect of light; the objects here lack the warm sparkle of later still lifes, or the subdued mystery of the *Still Life in a Cabinet.* But the power of this artist is rooted in his lack of pretense and the absence of desire to depict objects as prettier than he saw them.

PULZONE, SCIPIONE

b. Gaeta, (?)–d. Rome, 1598

Portrait of a Man–probably 1564

Oil on canvas, 43.5 x 34.5 cm.

The attribution of this portrait is uncertain; the writing in the dark background on the left, which reminds one of Pulzone, has become almost illegible. Moreover, the work is heavily damaged. Historians sometimes compare this painting with the work of Bronzino, and particularly of Moroni, because the portrait shows the great assurance and maturity of their work of the same period.

The critically observant expression of the eyes and the position of the head and the torso suggest that this is a self-portrait. The firmness and clarity of rendering make this work not only an extraordinary high point among Pulzone's somewhat flaccid work, but also a fine example of Italian painting in the late Renaissance.

COROT, JEAN BAPTISTE CAMILLE

b. Paris, 1796—d. Paris, 1875

View of Soissons—1833

Oil on canvas, 80 x 100 cm.

According to the commission given by a cloth manufacturer, Corot painted this landscape from the window of the former's office. Corot also painted this industrialist's house, the picture of which belongs to the collection of the Philadelphia Museum of Art.

There is a remarkable contrast between the rather conventional, almost eighteenth-century precision of the foreground and the expressive atmosphere of the background, in which we clearly recognize the later Corot. In the middle plane—the fields divided by little houses—the purity and sensitivity of Corot's approach manifest themselves. This approach is never emphatic or sentimental, but always full of an attentive respect for that which he depicts. More purely than any painter of his period, Corot succeeded in giving expression to the languid atmosphere of a summer afternoon in hazy, but never vague, forms and colors.

COROT

Young Woman at a Well—
    probably 1867

Oil on canvas, 65 x 42 cm.

This somewhat romantic painting was completed in the period when Corot was working on his series, *Young Woman in a Studio* (Louvre, Paris). It is possible that Corot used the same model both for this picture and for those of the series.

In this work, even more than in the later portraits influenced by Vermeer's hushed colors, Corot attained a fullness of tone that recalls Italian Renaissance painting. Central is the full color chord of green, wine-red, and golden yellow; the indeterminate background stresses this chromatic triad.

The model, posing in scenery reminiscent of old-fashioned photographs, has acquired, because of her somewhat artificial and immobile attitude, an inaccessible aloofness; her individuality reduced, our attention is now directed to the treatment of the color and material. Note particularly the girl's clothing, in which Corot seems to have become emotionally involved even though most of the painting was depicted objectively.

MILLET, JEAN FRANCOIS

b. Gruchy, 1814–d. Barbizon, 1875

A Woman Baking Bread—1854

Oil on canvas, 55 x 46 cm.

Vincent van Gogh admired Millet for the candid sincerity with which he depicted his models, mostly rustic people. That Millet did not romanticize his work can be seen by comparing *A Woman Baking Bread* with Corot's *Young Woman at a Well.* Millet, like Van Gogh, was highly sensitive to the relationship between the human being and his surroundings as well as to the gestures and attitudes of the individual in a work situation. His interest in such relationships can be associated with his concern for color relationship.

In 1848 Millet painted a baker shoving loaves into his oven. In 1854, the year when for the first time his material circumstances began improving due to the interest of some art collectors in his work, he painted *A Woman Baking Bread*, the companion piece. This picture, through intuition rather than rational planning, is highly balanced. The woman is completely incorporated into her surroundings because of the color chord; the vertical accent of the standing figure is counterbalanced by the axis running from the dough to the baskets on the floor. Such details as the light patches of the bonnet and the baskets are determined solely on the basis of symmetry.

FANTIN-LATOUR, HENRI

b. Grenoble, 1836–d. Buré, 1904

Still Life with Pears—1866

Oil on canvas, 73 x 58 cm.

Because of Mrs. Kröller's preference for Fantin-Latour's work, the Kröller-Müller Collection includes fifteen of his paintings, some drawings, and a large number of lithographs, the majority of which were purchased between 1913 and 1919.

Fantin-Latour had a "silent reverence for every occurrence"; he discovered beauty in such ordinary things as a small table knife or a saucer. Extremely delicate is his expressive rendering in this still life of the material of the nicely shaded, yet perfectly clear white tablecloth and the glossy pomegranates. The rims of the flowerpot and of the fruit dish soften the austere lines of the tabletop and the knife. Characteristic of Fantin-Latour's genius is the background in this work, rendered immaterial by its indefinable floating color.

FANTIN-LATOUR

Still Life with Strawberries—1867

Oil on canvas, 20.5 x 26.5 cm.

The intermingling of seeing, smelling, tasting, and touching is even greater in this small still life than in the more grandly conceived *Still Life with Pears*. By means of the color and the brush movement in his depiction of the strawberries and oranges, Fantin-Latour evokes almost palpable memories of sight, smell, touch, and taste.

The Belgian painter, De Braekeleer (1840-88), and the Dutch painter, Floris Verster (1861-1927)—who worked, like Fantin-Latour, in the quiet and isolated privacy of their homes—were perhaps the only ones, except Cézanne, who achieved on a small canvas a similar intensity of observation and intimate stillness in rendering.

MONTICELLI, ADOLPHE JOSEPH

b. Marseilles, 1824–d. Marseilles, 1886

Bouquet of Flowers—ca. 1875

Oil on panel, 52.5 x 33.5 cm.

Of Monticelli's work, Van Gogh wrote: "Monticelli sometimes made a bunch of flowers an excuse for gathering together in a single panel the whole range of his richest and most perfectly balanced tones....you must go straight to Delacroix to find anything equal to his orchestration of colors." Monticelli's autonomous, almost abstract, use of sparkling colors is a unique phenomenon in his time.

After a stay in Paris, where he especially admired the works of Delacroix and Rembrandt, Monticelli traveled on foot to the South of France when the Franco-Prussian War broke out in 1870. In 1871 he reached Marseilles, his native city, where he was to stay for the rest of his life. An anecdote tells that he locked himself up in his room and worked like one possessed—in the night by the light of a candle, and in the daytime in a dusky room, the red curtains tightly closed.

RENOIR, PIERRE AUGUSTE

b. Limoges, 1841–d. Cagnes, 1919

The Clown—1868

Oil on canvas, 193.5 x 130 cm.

The Clown, an early Renoir painting, was probably intended as a poster for the café of the *"Cirque d'Hiver"* in Paris. The clown, John Price, was very famous in his time.

A somewhat academic inhibition is apparent in both the composition and the rendering of the clown. The transparent, free touch, characteristic of the late Renoir, can be seen only in the clown's hair and in the little figures in the box.

This picture is one of the favorites in the Kröller-Müller collection, probably because it so strongly evokes the atmosphere of the circus and the *"café-chantant."* This is the environment in which Renoir's generation, and the younger one to which Toulouse-Lautrec belonged, so much liked to tarry, and which still represents to us of the twentieth century the entrancing atmosphere of the *belle époque*.

RENOIR

The Café—1876

Oil on canvas, 35 x 28 cm.

Painted during the culminating period of impressionism, this work shows most of the characteristics of that style: the free, sketchy touch, the delicate nuances, the atmosphere vibrating with light and shade, and the indeterminate activities of people. All this indicates the impressionists' deep conviction that all living things breathe, grow, and change.

Unique to Renoir was his reaction to the hands and the small lifted face of the actress, Jeanne Samary. Unlike his fellow-artists Monet and Pissarro, Renoir rarely made the random coming and going of an anonymous group the subject of his pictures. Only his friends, united in an atmosphere of intimacy, led him to take up the brush.

By depicting two men looking in opposite directions, Renoir subtly evokes unlimited space in front of as well as behind the central plane. Such depth is again seen in the left part of the panel where the art critic, Georges Rivière—the enjoying eye—and the two women have been placed in one group, while the painter, Frédéric Cordley—the contemplating eye—turns away and to the right. Renoir depicts a vague background that is not a plane, but still gives an impression of depth.

MONET, CLAUDE

b. Paris, 1840—d. Giverny, 1926

The Studio Boat—1874

Oil on canvas, 50 x 64 cm.

The impressionists were the first painters who planned and finished their landscapes in the open air. To study the changeable interplay of light and shade on the spot, Monet—following the example of the Barbizon painter, Daubigny—had a studio boat built. Like no other, Monet knew how to picture the deceptive relation of the human being and his shadow, of the object and its reflection. The line of limitation between water and land, solid and liquid, and inhabited and uninhabited were subjects highly cherished by the impressionists.

In *The Studio Boat* Monet creates depth by turning the boat's opening toward us. Also, he crosses the horizontal composition with a clearly visible diagonal that darts into the depth via the boat to the isolated group of the tree and the house at the left. This is characteristic of the impressionists' attempt to break through the limitation of the painted plane and the frame of the picture.

SISLEY, ALFRED

b. Paris, 1839–d. Moret-sur-Loing, 1899

The Brickfield—1880

Oil on canvas, 37 x 55.5 cm.

Like Monet, Sisley was greatly stimulated during a trip to London by the watercolors of Turner, Bonington, and Constable. He himself painted mostly landscapes, the majority of which he did near the Seine. In this borderland between water and land, it was not so much the movement of the river and the fluttering of the leaves that fascinated him as the atmosphere, saturated with vapor, which rendered the shapes shadowy and the colors indistinct.

Occasionally Sisley's paintings show a certain languor that may have been a result of his poor health and his financial difficulties; the family estate had dwindled away during the Franco-Prussian War. *The Brickfield*, however, has much directness: the excited, smooth movement of the brush and the bright colors create a fluorescent sincerity rarely so prominent in Sisley's work. The somewhat melancholy aloofness, characteristic of many of his paintings, has completely disappeared. Outstanding are the sailing clouds and the sweeping movement of the trees and the field. The small patches of red in this predominantly green and blue composition help to increase the feeling of motion.

CÉZANNE, PAUL

b. Aix-en-Provence, 1839–
d. Aix-en-Provence, 1906

Road Leading to a Lake—ca. 1890

Oil on canvas, 92 x 75 cm.

An environment brought to life by human beings, the delight of the impressionists, was for Cézanne, their contemporary, an obstacle. This obstacle delayed the full expression of his creative potential.

Cézanne was at his best before a landscape, fruit, or a human being whose existence was felt quite apart from his own. His subjects have their own self-communing personality to the extent that it seems as if the painter depicted them with an increasingly more penetrating observation of their structure. Through his subjective surrender to what he experienced as absolutely objective themes, Cézanne created a lifework to which the terms "subjective" and "objective" can no longer be applied: he effaced the borderline between them.

VAN GOGH, VINCENT WILLEM

b. Zundert, 1853–d. Auvers-sur-Oise,
1890

Young Girl in a Wood—September 1882

Oil on canvas, 39 x 59 cm.

In 1882 Van Gogh worked for a time in the studio of his uncle Anton Mauve, a landscape painter. There he received technical advice and did watercolors and small oil paintings, of which *Young Girl in a Wood* was one of the first. The daring and confident brushwork of this canvas is remarkable for a novice at oil painting.

One of the English prints that Van Gogh collected portrayed a little figure dressed in white, standing alone in an autumnal wood. Greatly attracted to this theme, Van Gogh repeatedly introduced variations on it into the work he did at The Hague and later in France. At the later period he seldom rendered his models in colors that contrast them with the surroundings; he almost invariably saw the color and form of the human being wholly absorbed by the landscape. While at The Hague, Van Gogh's power of expression grew. Through his painting in oils he became conscious of, among other things, the function of light.

VAN GOGH

Interior with Weaver—July 1884

Oil on canvas, 62 x 93 cm.

A pictorial problem that concerned Van Gogh while he was at Nuenen finds expression in this picture: how to depict a human being working busily in a dimly lighted room. The construction of the loom and the worker's identification with his tool intrigued Van Gogh. He was greatly impressed by the extent to which weavers and peasants seemed inexorably chained to their work.

With a tenacity so characteristic of him, he repeated this theme in oil, watercolor, ink, and crayon, until he had mastered the technique. As a result he made, within three months, nine paintings and seventeen drawings of weavers. The following year he concentrated exclusively on rendering a peasant family in a dark cottage, eating their dinner by the light of a paraffin lamp.

VAN GOGH

Head of a Peasant Woman in a White Cap—April 1885

Oil on canvas, 44 x 36 cm.

Head of a Peasant Woman in a White Cap is one of the preliminary studies Van Gogh made for his great painting, *The Potato Eaters.* In this work he principally sought after pure truth, even though he believed that an honest rendering of what he saw and experienced as the essential being of these people would probably be offensive to others.

As early as this period of his career, Van Gogh was convinced that by using murky colors and by applying paint in a strong impasto with angular brushstrokes, he would not distort the image of these people, but would express their peculiar worth and their "quite different way of life." He totally rejected the literary heroism, the somewhat condescending compassion, and the purely pictorial approach of many nineteenth-century artists; in his pictures he tried to express an unsentimental, objective respect.

VAN GOGH

Autumnal Landscape with Four Trees
    —November 1885

Oil on canvas, 64 x 89 cm.

Autumnal Landscape with Four Trees was painted a few weeks before Van Gogh left Holland for France via Belgium. In this large picture Van Gogh's growth as a painter between 1882 and 1885 can be seen. Comparing this work to *Young Girl in a Wood*, notable developments include the delicate nuances of the colors, the greater differentiation of space, and the power of transmitting mood to the spectator. The light touches of lively rhythm recall the white highlighting often seen in Van Gogh's drawings.

The motif of the leafless tree standing somewhat apart from the others of rich foliage is strongly effective. The tree, as a symbolic theme, reappears in Van Gogh's work as a willow, a pine tree, a fruit tree, or a cypress. At times it is bare, at other times storm-beaten. Often two trees stand so close that their branches become intertwined, possibly symbolic of Van Gogh's deep attachment to his younger brother Theo.

VAN GOGH

Red Herrings—1886

Oil on canvas, 45 x 37 cm.

Red Herrings is one of a large series of still lifes and flower pieces painted during Van Gogh's first year in Paris. As an early work, its coloring is dark and its brushstrokes show a thick impasto, similar to that of Van Gogh's work in Holland. The deep blue and the warm golden lines of light foreshadow the bright blue and yellow characteristic of Van Gogh's mature style. Interesting is the fiery red signature, "Vincent," that stands out brightly against the dark background.

Van Gogh did several versions of this still life of red herrings, typical of his frequent returns to a few principal themes. Sometimes these reiterations resulted from his desire to give not only to Theo, but also to his mother and to his friends, an idea of his progress.

VAN GOGH

The Mill "le Radet"—June-July 1886
Oil on canvas, 37 x 45 cm.

The mill depicted here stood close to the house in which Vincent and Theo lived in Montmartre. In France, as in Holland, Van Gogh became familiar with his surroundings by fixing their image in paintings and drawings. Consequently, he painted several views from the windows of his apartment.

In this painting, done during Vincent's first months in Paris, the light is beginning to break through and the color is becoming brighter. The touches of blue, the free movement of the brush, the lively, ornamental symbols of the letters, and the small paving stones distributed over the surface impart a vital energy to this well-balanced composition. While working on *The Mill*, Van Gogh wrote in a letter to a friend: "Trying to render intense color," and "I have faith in color." (Letter 459a)

The image of Vincent as a "painter possessed," a self-taught artistic adventurer who freed himself of his inner tensions in his work, is contradicted by his letters, which show how systematically he occupied himself with the problem of pictorial technique.

VAN GOGH

Self-Portrait—1887

Oil on paper, 32 x 23 cm.

In Paris Van Gogh painted at least twenty small self-portraits, resulting from his need to confront himself. In this *Self-Portrait* the touches of hatching and the bright blue-green and reddish colors show the influences of the French Impressionists. Unique to Van Gogh, however, is the intensity resulting from the searching look, the concentration of the yellow and blue colors in the beard and the cravat, the variability of the handling of the brush, and the powerful tracing of some of the contours. Such intensity, the core of Van Gogh's individuality, remained even in the periods when he dealt with the same pictorial problems that concerned his contemporaries.

VAN GOGH

Interior of a Restaurant—1887

Oil on canvas, 45 x 54 cm.

Interior of a Restaurant is the best example of Van Gogh's temporary and partial assimilation of divisionism, a technique initiated by Seurat and followed by Signac. Rarely are his colors so delicate and exquisite. Freeing himself from the constraining precision of the divisionist method, Van Gogh interspersed the round dots with short curved touches. Varied also is the perspective as seen at the right. Other French painters would hardly have painted a café without people, but the top hat is the only indication of human presence in this work.

Signac was one of Van Gogh's most loyal friends; they often worked together in the surroundings of Paris. The close relationship of working methods in several pictures by Signac and Van Gogh makes it impossible to decide which of the two was artistically the giver and which the receiver. The great change that took place in Van Gogh's work in 1887 is largely attributable to his contact with Signac.

VAN GOGH

Sunflowers—Summer 1887

Oil on canvas, 60 x 100 cm.

Sunflowers is one of the most dramatic works from Van Gogh's Paris period. The style is hardly characteristic of this period; however, because several other versions of this motif all date from 1887, it is more than likely that this work was executed at the same time. In 1888, in Arles, Vincent returned to the sunflower theme to embellish the room he had reserved for his friend Gauguin. The sunflowers in these later paintings, unlike the ones here, were in a vase and in full bloom.

Both the sun and the sunflower were symbols of love to Van Gogh. It is possible that the present picture was painted at the time Van Gogh felt the need to give up living with Theo, because the tension of Paris life had become unbearable to him. By comparing this still life with *Red Herrings*, painted more than a year earlier, we clearly see that while in Paris Van Gogh freed himself of all academicism. The background, charged with his emotional reactions, particularly represents this change.

VAN GOGH

Pastureland—1887

Oil on canvas, 31.5 x 40.5

The feather-light, regular touch, the delicate colors, and the concentration on one small spot of a vernal meadow indicate that Van Gogh painted *Pastureland* at a time when he felt relaxed and happy. His quiet interest in the smallest detail can be traced to the Japanese prints he collected.

Van Gogh explored the spirit of the Japanese art of drawing as intensely as he had studied English graphic art. Like Hokusai and Hiroshige, Van Gogh could show his rich artistic talent in every small detail. He admired their subtle admixture of contrasts that alluded to the fullness of life not as a struggle of contradictory elements, but as an essential mutual enrichment.

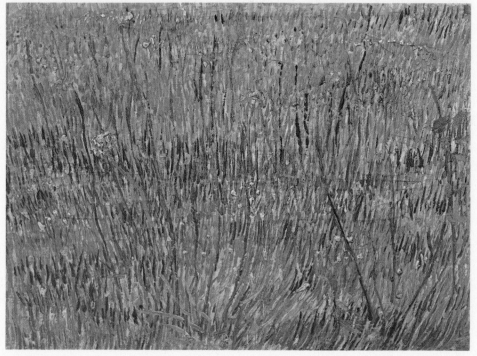

VAN GOGH

Still Life with Apples in a Basket—
    Autumn 1887

Oil on canvas, 50 x 61 cm.

In Paris, as well as later in Arles, Vincent searched for a "more abstract" background closely related to his subjects, in this case a basket with apples. He also tried to free himself from the traditional fixed viewpoint of the artist.

The fluency of Van Gogh's brush as seen in *Still Life with Apples in a Basket,* shows to what extent his manner of painting is related to his drawing technique. Gradually, he came to paint more graphically, that is, more like the way he drew. In these same years his means of graphic expression, little dots and dashes, commas, and curves, acquired an almost inexhaustible richness and variation.

à l'ami Lucien Pissaro
Vincent

VAN GOGH

Orchard Surrounded by Cypresses—
        April 1888

Oil on canvas, 65 x 81 cm.

In February 1888, on the advice of Toulouse-Lautrec, Van Gogh moved to Arles, "the land of the blue tones and the gay colors." Upon his arrival there he found snow on the ground, but everywhere the fruit trees had begun to blossom. Enraptured with the landscape and the clear light, he painted one orchard after the other for three weeks at a stretch.

The division of space in *Orchard Surrounded by Cypresses* is reminiscent of some of the drawings done in Holland. The problem of space occupied Van Gogh's mind constantly, and during the first weeks in Arles he used a perspective frame, as he had in The Hague.

Van Gogh also gave much thought to "a complete decorative scheme," a whole series of works devoted to the same theme. This idea of making decorative series was only fully realized by the generation of Vuillard, even though it dated back to the impressionists, notably in such series as Monet's *Waterlilies.* That Van Gogh also wanted to make triptychs, and that he indicated how he wanted his pictures framed, show his concern for the function of art in the daily life and environment of the average man.

VAN GOGH

Still Life with Lemons and Bottle—
    May 1888

Oil on canvas, 53 x 63 cm.

During the first weeks at Arles, when it was still too cold to work outdoors the entire day, Van Gogh worked on a series of still lifes.

The foundation of *Still Life with Lemons and Bottle* seems more concrete than that of *Still Life with Apples in a Basket*. The corner of the table serves to create a clear triangular relationship between the orange and lemon that lie apart from the basket and the bottle.

The refined green of the background recalls the gold of the Byzantines and the pure blue of Fra Angelico, both used to indicate an unearthly, celestial space. There is a difference in the movement of the brush between the almost stippled background and the firmer, more palpable stroke of the foreground.

VAN GOGH

View of Saintes-Maries—June 1888

Oil on canvas, 64 x 53 cm.

In June Van Gogh took the stagecoach to Saintes-Maries on the Mediterranean coast, where he stayed for a week. His frequently spoken references to Cézanne preceding this trip confirm the structural relationship of this painting to Cézanne's canvases. Seen in this painting are Van Gogh's extremely keen eye, his sensitivity to atmosphere and color, and the quickness with which he absorbed totally new surroundings in detail.

Of Saintes-Maries, Van Gogh wrote to his brother Theo: "I wish you could spend some time here, you would feel it after a while, one's sight changes: you see things with an eye more Japanese, you feel color differently. The Japanese draw quickly, very quickly, like a lightning flash, because their nerves are finer, their feelings simpler." (Letter 500)

VAN GOGH

Haystacks in Provence—June 1888

Oil on canvas, 73 x 92 cm.

"Just now we are having a glorious strong heat, with no wind, just what I want. There is a sun, a light that for want of a better word I can only call yellow, pale sulphur yellow, pale golden citron. How lovely yellow is!" (Letter 522) These words help to explain the radiant vigor of this painting.

The taut, straight touch, now compressed into a tissue of horizontal and vertical dashes, creates a feeling of vehemence in the sky over the haystack on the right, not found in the work of Arles. Such spots recur in the works of this period, giving to inanimate and natural objects an expressive value reserved by most painters for human models.

VAN GOGH

The Sower—Summer 1888
Oil on canvas, 64 x 80.5 cm.

The figure of a sower is a major motif in Van Gogh's work; between 1880 and 1890 he devoted twenty-five drawings and seven paintings to it. Van Gogh expressed his feelings on this subject in a letter written in 1889: "I feel so strongly that it is the same with people as with wheat; if you are not sown in the earth to germinate there, what does it matter?—in the end you are ground between the millstones to become bread." (Letter 607) Van Gogh repeatedly struggled with a deep-rooted doubt about the value of his life and work, a doubt balanced, however, by his wholehearted acceptance of life.

Other letters written about this picture reveal Van Gogh's principal preoccupation as the emotional value of the colors. The sun in this work is closely related to the image of the sower. It appears here, for the first time, as a large round disk, connecting the house on the left to the sower.

Stylistically, this picture recalls Van Gogh's *Pastureland* and *Café in Paris*, particularly the abrupt, draughtsmanly brushstrokes and the broken colors divided into the complementary blue, mauve, and yellow. The high line of the horizon, imparting an emotional value to the ruggedly plowed earth, divides the sower in half—one part belonging to the earth and its unreaped grain, the other to the wheat-colored sky.

VAN GOGH

Café Terrace at Night (Place du Forum)
      —September 1888

Oil on canvas, 81 x 65.5 cm.

In September of 1888 Van Gogh was occupied with the problem of rendering the night and the night sky. To him the deep blue of the night sky, the stars, and the moon were symbols of human love and affection; he wanted to reflect this in his nocturnal landscapes.

Café Terrace at Night is divided both horizontally and vertically. There is a separation between the tables and chairs in the foreground which are unoccupied, and the small tables in the background at which a few people sit. There is also a separation between the café platform lined by empty tables and the cobblestone street. The colors, although of enormous intensity, balance each other.

When this picture was executed, Van Gogh, no longer enraptured by the South, doubted his ability to depict his strong emotions. He was furnishing his little house and pressing Gauguin to come and share it.

VAN GOGH

Portrait of Milliet—September 1888

Oil on canvas, 60 x 49 cm.

Milliet, one of Van Gogh's friends in Arles, was a second lieutenant of the Zouaves; the star and crescent in the upper right-hand corner appear on the badge of his regiment. Van Gogh admired Milliet for his casual way of life and his manner with women. Together they wandered about the country, and Van Gogh gave Milliet drawing lessons. Van Gogh hung this portrait of Milliet in his bedroom along with the one he made of his friend, Emile Boch.

The red shako and the pink color of the ears and the mouth contrast with the sallow complexion of the face and the deep green of the background. Another remarkable contrast is found between the stringent, almost two-dimensional treatment of the figure and the agitated relief of the background.

VAN GOGH

Willows at Sunset—October 1888

Oil on cardboard, 31 x 34 cm.

Delacroix had set the example of seeking, outside of Paris, a reinvigoration for his work; Cézanne, Van Gogh, Gauguin, and others of the postimpressionists followed his example.

If we compare this vigorous little landscape to those of Sisley or Monet, we can more clearly understand what Van Gogh meant when he wrote to Gauguin: "It will even be necessary for me to recover somewhat more from the stultifying influence of our so-called civilization in order to have a better model for a better picture....I forget everything in favor of the external beauty of things, which I cannot reproduce, for in my pictures I render it as something ugly and coarse, whereas nature seems perfect to me. However, at present the *élan* of my bony carcass is such that it goes straight for its goal. The result of this is a sincerity, perhaps original at times, in what I feel, if only the subject can lend something to my rash and clumsy execution." (Letter 544a)

VAN GOGH

Portrait of a Man—probably
November 1888

Oil on canvas, 65 x 54.5 cm.

Van Gogh probably painted this portrait about the same time he did *Boy with the Cap* (Nathan Collection, Zurich) and the portrait of Armand Roulin (Folkwang Museum, Essen), shortly after Gauguin had finally joined him at Arles. This picture, called *Portrait of an Actor* for a long time, was mistakenly thought to have been the portrait of a patient in St. Rémy, and thus executed at a later date.

Van Gogh probably never rendered a portrait with such an expressionistic and tense head and with such a singular torsion of the axis of the face. It is believed that Van Gogh, when he painted this portrait, was already in a state of great inner tension. This tension, and his highly emotional approach to his model, explain Van Gogh's identification with the extreme vulnerability of his sitter.

VAN GOGH

Les Alyscamps—November 1888

Oil on canvas, 73 x 92 cm.

In none of Van Gogh's works is Gauguin's influence so clearly visible as in *Les Alyscamps*. Les Alyscamps, originally Elysii Campi, was a pre-Christian cemetery, later used by the Christians. Gauguin made it the subject of some pictures and Van Gogh painted it repeatedly. Although Van Gogh gave a very lucid description of this work in letters to Theo, to his sister, and to his friend Bernard, there are no indications that he was conscious of the stylistic change it represented, notable in the remarkably high viewpoint, the flat touch, the decorative disposition of the colors, and the filling of the plane.

Later, at St. Rémy, he wrote that under Gauguin's influence he had twice "let myself go to an abstraction," once with *Woman Reading Novels* and again with *La Berceuse (Woman in a Rocking Chair)*. Examination of these works reveals that "abstraction" meant to Van Gogh a freedom from the actual colors of objects and an unrestricted surrender to the symbolism of colors. Van Gogh would not have considered *Les Alyscamps* an abstraction, because he saw a marked difference between manipulation of color for aesthetic effect, as in *Les Alyscamps*, and a conscious use of symbolic colors, as in *La Berceuse*.

VAN GOGH

The Postman Roulin—
        February-March 1889

Oil on canvas, 65 x 54 cm.

By the end of December 1888, the conflict that had been brewing for weeks between Van Gogh and Gauguin came to a head. Vincent was taken to a hospital and Gauguin returned to Paris. When Van Gogh returned home, the postman, a longtime friend whose portrait he had painted several times in the summer of 1888, proved to be one of his few friends. Milliet had left for Africa in November. Toward the end of January Roulin was transferred to Marseilles, and his family followed him a month later. Of Roulin, Van Gogh wrote: "Roulin, though he is not old enough to be like a father to me, has nevertheless a silent gravity and a tenderness for me such as an old soldier might have for a young one." (Letter 583)

There have been many hypotheses as to the meaning of the flowery background and the ornamentally stylized undulations of Roulin's beard in this portrait. Since neither of these characteristics appeared in the portraits Van Gogh did of Roulin before his illness, it is likely that this portrait was done when Roulin returned to spend a weekend with his family before their final move to Marseilles.

VAN GOGH

Olive Grove—Summer 1889

Oil on canvas, 72 x 92 cm.

In May 1889, with his full consent, Van Gogh was taken to an asylum in St. Rémy. He realized that he was no longer capable of living by himself. During the first months there he often had to stay indoors but in the summer he resumed his large landscape studies. He wrote about the olive gardens to a friend in Holland: "The effect of daylight, of the sky, makes it possible to extract an infinity of subjects from the olive tree. Now, I on my part sought contrasting effects in the foliage, changing with the hues of the sky. At times the whole is a pure all-pervading blue, namely when the tree bears its pale flowers, and big blue flies, emerald rose beetles and cicadas in great numbers are hovering around it...." (Letter 614a)

The undulating movement of *Olive Grove,* so characteristic of Van Gogh's work in St. Rémy, unites the earth, the trees, and the sky into a single stream without affecting the volume of the trees. Notwithstanding his state of mind, Van Gogh created a spiritually scintillating work through the transparent silver-blue of the sky, the diaphanous green of the trees, and the subtly shaded, delicate colors of the earth.

VAN GOGH

Wheatfield, Reaper, and Sun—
   June-September 1889

Oil on canvas, 72 x 92 cm.

"There! The Reaper is finished. I think it will be one of those you keep at home—it is an image of death as the great book of nature speaks of it, but what I have sought is the 'almost smiling.' It is all yellow except a line of violet hills, a pale fair yellow. I find it queer that I saw it like this from between the iron bars of a cell." (Letter 604) This description reveals much of Van Gogh's feelings and thoughts during the months at St. Rémy: his lucid awareness of the fragility of his creative power, and the unending struggle to turn his awareness into serene wisdom.

The sun and the sky appear as inseparable as the reaper and the wheat, all depicted in the same full yellow. Only the brush movement differentiates between the elements within this totality.

Wheatfield, Reaper and Sun, a companion piece to *The Sower,* symbolized for Van Gogh both the loneliness of life and the acceptance of it with its inseparable element, death.

VAN GOGH

Haystack under a Rainy Sky—n.d.

Oil on canvas, 63 x 52 cm.

It is difficult to date this work. The broken colors and the formation of the clouds suggest that it was painted at St. Rémy. However, the pronounced yellow–blue contrast recalls Van Gogh's Arles period, in which *The Sower* was executed. This contrast also recalls one of Van Gogh's letters: "...I am always in hope of making a discovery there (in the study of color), to express the love of two lovers by a wedding of two complementary colors, their mingling and their opposition, the mysterious vibrations of kindred tones." (Letter 531)

Seldom did Van Gogh oppose the colors blue and yellow so decidedly: as image and reflected image and as object and shadow, the yellow in a full voluminous form and the blue as an abstracting ornamental reflection. The blue itself defies determination: is it a sheet of water or is it the shadow of the haystack?

VAN GOGH

*Evening in the Park of St. Paul's
Hospital*—November 1889

Oil on canvas, 60 x 49 cm.

While he was in St. Rémy, Van Gogh's colors became progressively more differentiated, and the movement of his brush changed. The colors—particularly the green—show at times an unprecedented, almost aggressive intensity, and at other times an utter sadness.

In *Evening in the Park of St. Paul's Hospital* the circling brush movements and the singularly steep course of the road are arrested by the plaiting of crisscross brushstrokes at the bottom of the picture. Because of her blue and twisted form, like that of the tree, the figure is completely absorbed by the surrounding landscape. She seems to have lost her identity. The open frontal plane, the road that comes streaming down like a cataract, and the background fenced in by a row of trees are characteristic of many pictures that Van Gogh completed at St. Rémy. The short curves that look like waves toppling over—seen here at the bottom right—also appear often in the drawings and paintings of this period.

VAN GOGH

The Enclosed Field—March-April 1890

Oil on canvas, 72 x 92 cm.

The division of space and the merciless green color of the young wheat in *The Enclosed Field* show once again that Van Gogh was a lone wolf among contemporary artists. The block of horizontal and vertical strokes and the strip of wild flowers act as a dam to the steep, downward-sloping field. There is also an inclination, possibly a Japanese influence, to break from a fixed viewpoint through the almost riotous structure of the painting.

By means of parallel brushstrokes and a nicely balanced distribution of kindred colors, Van Gogh succeeded in creating a firm organization in this field loaded with energy. The manner in which he rendered the treetops, as two halves of a fruit, is typical of his style during his last months at St. Rémy and the weeks he lived in Auvers.

VAN GOGH

*Mountainous Landscape near
    St. Rémy*—March-April 1890

Oil on canvas, 59 x 72 cm.

Van Gogh saw these mountains—rendered here as close, interlocking wedges—from his hospital window. The intense blue and green are relieved by the delicate areas of ochre and mauve. The white of the clouds and the mountains is strongly emphasized. More than ever the tension, and the will to control this tension, are perceptible in the heavy outlines and the violent contrasts.

An appreciative article, by the young art critic Albert Aurier, published in January 1890, had greatly excited Van Gogh. Delighted by this expert's response to his work, he became less fearful of being unable to achieve the image constantly in his mind. In the same month Theo's son was born, and Van Gogh felt even more guilty over the continual sacrifices Theo had to make in order to support him financially.

VAN GOGH

Road with Cypress and Star—May 1890

Oil on canvas, 92 x 73 cm.

Road with Cypress and Star is probably one of the last pictures Van Gogh painted at St. Rémy; he later had it sent to himself in Auvers, where he spent the last two months of his life. From Auvers he wrote to Gauguin about this work; his letter contains a little sketch, different in two essential points from the picture: the curious spot of shadow, like a wedge in the stream of the road, is missing and the cypress has only a single trunk. These corrections helped Van Gogh to dissociate himself rationally from the emotional deformations of the canvas.

The motif of the "pair" dominates the picture: there are two laborers, a man and a woman in the tilt-cart, the moon and the star, and so on. The cypress leaps up like a black flame and separates the inhabited world—house, cart, and laborers—from the dramatic landscape.

VAN GOGH

The Good Samaritan (after Delacroix)
—May 1890

Oil on canvas, 72 x 59 cm.

Too ill to work in the open air, Van Gogh painted in his room from engravings sent to him by Theo. Millet, Delacroix, and Rembrandt particularly fascinated him. About these copies Van Gogh wrote to Theo: "Many people do not copy, many others do—I started on it accidentally, and I find that it teaches me things, and above all it sometimes gives me consolation. And then my brush goes between my fingers as a bow would on the violin, and absolutely for my own pleasure." (Letter 607)

In the center of *The Good Samaritan,* the almost sculptural block of the Samaritan stands near the Wayfarer, painted in blue, yellow, red, and reddish brown. The figures are surrounded by the flowing forms of the landscape, painted in broken colors derived from these fundamentals. The head of the Samaritan may be a self-portrait.

The subject, the quotation, the broken melancholy colors, and the unconcerned little figure going up the path on the left—probably a symbol of the outside world—all allude to Van Gogh's intense feelings of loneliness.

SEURAT, GEORGES

b. Paris, 1859—d. Paris, 1891

Harbor Entrance at Honfleur—1886

Oil on canvas, 46 x 55 cm.

Whenever we feel inclined to reduce all artists of a single generation to the same stylistic denominator, pictures like this one contain an unmistakable hint to drop the idea definitely. Is it possible to imagine greater contrasts than those between Van Gogh and Seurat, two representatives of one generation? And yet, light and color and space occupied the minds of both. But how different were their approaches! Van Gogh, working in a blazing sun (which he enjoyed "like a cricket"), sought colors that are "comforting like music," based as much on emotional associations as on observation; on the other hand Seurat, to whom it was quite immaterial whether he painted by the light of day or by gaslight, tried to analyze colors in order to find their purest scientifically calculated components.

Whereas in Seurat's later works the underlayer of each painting is entirely covered with the tiny round touches of color, the colors of this harbor view seem almost to be strained through the vapor of the water, and immaterialized under the influence of the nacre-like tissue beneath. By giving life to a membrane of paint, covered with gossamer lightness, Seurat succeeded in realizing what the impressionists preceding him had been searching for: the mutual penetration of light and color.

SEURAT

A Corner of the Harbor of Honfleur—
      1886

Oil on canvas, 79.5 x 63 cm.

The object of Seurat's method (divisionism) was to get, by means of breaking up colors into their components, an optically clearer picture than was possible by mixing the colors on the palette. The starting point was therefore the interaction, or rather the interpenetration, of complementary colors.

What had been to Delacroix and Van Gogh a revelation discovered while painting, was thought out by Seurat down to the minutest details. This interaction is operative not only on the colors as such, but also on the power of the colors: a light color becomes lighter, a dark color darker in consequence of adjacent contrasts. Thus the short round touch is not fundamental to this method, as the often-used term "pointillism" (from the French *point,* "dot") might suggest, but is rather its final result. Seurat's investigation of the relationship and interaction between light and shade and between complementary colors was almost a logical consequence of his extremely refined perception of the mutual influence exercised by tone and form, already developed in the drawings of the year before he turned to painting (1881-82).

In contemplating the picture reproduced here, if we start from the accented lines and planes and follow the design in its gradations, it becomes clear how closely Seurat approaches pure abstraction. We can also understand his preference for such clearly constructed, simple objects as lighthouses, jetties, and unspectacular houses, whose aesthetic and emotional effect is based exclusively on their unimpeded perceptibility.

SEURAT

Sunday at Port-en-Bessin—1888

Oil on canvas, 66 x 82 cm.

This harbor view—with its wealth of contrasts in color, line, tone, and living and "dead" things—must have been to the artist something like a touchstone for the potency of his method.

Every force finds a counterforce. The most mobile elements, flags waving in the wind, walking people, and swaying boats, are congealed to an almost purely ornamental function. The most sterile elements, a wooden railing, a mast, an utterly drab house, are almost brought to life. And a simple construction of horizontals, verticals, and diagonals gains complexity because of tiny displacements.

Even the intellectual sophistication of Seurat's subtle discipline does not let us forget for a moment what was probably the origin of this never-ceasing striving after reconciliation: the personality of the artist himself (which may be read in his drawings even more clearly than in his paintings), an artist who in his vulnerable and nervous oversensitiveness created the image of a breathless happiness, to which the melancholy awareness of transiency lent a creative tension.

SEURAT ·

The Chahut—1889-90

Oil on canvas, 169 x 139 cm.

Even more than the preceding picture, *The Chahut* proves that a purely "pictorial" space, which has height and width but no depth, is the logical consequence of Seurat's search for an image that conforms to the scientific rules of harmony rather than to everyday reality. Depth, which must become unfathomable and break away from the artist's orderly planning, is thus suppressed. But how fragile the artist's desire is for the absolutely pure artefact of two dimensions is proved by the luminous patches of the gas lamps, which in themselves *evoke* depth and perforate the compactness of the back wall.

The gesture of the conductor seems powerless and superfluous before the proud approach of the dancers. But are they really dancers, or are they animated ornaments that imitate and ridicule the motions of human beings? We might, perhaps, at least believe in the imperturbable presence of the bass player, except that his affectedly raised finger, as well as his ornamentally symmetrical connection with the conductor to the left and the farcical spectator to the right, incorporate him too in their artificial world, and estrange him from ours. After the water-clear blue-green of Port-en-Bessin, Seurat's colors have become indescribably complicated.

Mrs. Kröller bought this canvas at the urgent advice of Henri van de Velde, and always wanted to have it near her.

SIGNAC, PAUL

b. Paris, 1863—d. Paris, 1935

The Breakfast—1886-87

Oil on canvas, 89 x 115 cm.

When he was twenty-one years old, Signac became an ardent follower of Georges Seurat. Like Seurat he chose his themes from the same orbit as did the impressionists but, at times even more coolly than Seurat himself, he placed his figures and landscapes in a state of timeless isolation. After 1888 the tension in Signac's work diminished, and the pictures painted after Seurat's death clearly show to what extent Signac had to curb his own exuberant nature in order to apply Seurat's method so conscientiously and intelligently.

This picture of Signac's parents, in which the master of the house ostensibly dominates, actually gives the most forceful accent to the female figure because of the light recess of the window and the pronounced vertical from the aspidistra to the decanter on the table. It is fascinating to observe how Signac, notwithstanding the accurate application of divisionism and the echoes—especially in the female figures—of Seurat's work, has reached a perfectly personal monumentality, in which light and dark colors are brought to an absolute equilibrium.

SIGNAC

Harbor of Collioure—1887

Oil on canvas, 33 x 46 cm.

Signac, a passionate yachtsman, repeatedly cruised along the coasts of the Mediterranean and was in Collioure in the fall of 1887. He painted studies in the open air, and then, in his studio, developed them into finished works. His harbor views are among his most charming works, avoiding the tenseness of his figure pieces. Revealing a perfectly natural handling of impressionistic elements (as, for instance, the cutting of the little boats to the left), these generally small canvases surprise us by their fluency, their delicate colors, and their open composition.

P. Signac. 87   Op. 164

ENSOR, JAMES

b. Ostende, 1860–d. Ostende, 1949

Still Life with Blue Jug—1890

Oil on panel, 38 x 46 cm.

This still life was painted at a time when Ensor still had his full creative power at his disposal. There is a magnificence about the arrangement of the warm red, the blue, and the green, with broken tints in between. The thin, twirly lines, which after 1892 often lose themselves in a capricious overgrowth, here have a perfectly valid, playful function, even in the metalwork on the ear of the jug (where, however, we see something of the ambiguity of form that was to become characteristic of Ensor's later "mannerism," as caustic as it was evasive). Ensor's palette here still has an unprecedented abundance of iridescent colors, and the red and pink are still quite free of the almost furtive harshness of the later period. A remarkable dialogue is carried on between the jug and the candlestick and between the two wineglasses—a dialogue in color, form, and expressive value.

DENIS, MAURICE

b. Granville, 1870–d. Paris, 1943

April—1892

Oil on canvas, 37.5 x 61 cm.

In his writings Maurice Denis gave a lucid synopsis of all the wishes and ideas of the *Nabis,* a group that was greatly stimulated by the work Gauguin did in his Breton period. The guide to his work is to be found in the formula that a painting is pre-eminently *"une surface plane recouverte de couleurs en un ordre assemblés"* (a flat surface covered with colors assembled in a certain order).

Later Denis' own creative power weakened somewhat, and his admiration for the Italian fresco painters, as well as his great erudition, acted as a restraint upon his spontaneity. Then at times his color became sugary and lost its sparkle. The recognition of the aesthetic primacy, expressed in Denis' revolutionary formula, then degenerated into an a-vital aestheticism.

REDON, ODILON

b. Bordeaux, 1840–d. Paris, 1916

Pegasus Triumphant—1905-7

Oil on cardboard, 47 x 63 cm.

For years Redon's works were dominated by the motif of Pegasus, the winged horse of imagination. In 1889 it appears shackled and powerlessly struggling; after 1900 Pegasus, as the artist, triumphs over the monster that is the image of all strangling forces in the outer world and in the artist himself. The horse itself, especially the fighting horse, was a favorite symbol for Romantic artists such as Delacroix, Eugène Fromentin, Chassériau, Géricault, as was the centaur for such later artists as Gustave Moreau, uniting the opposing forces in a single personality.

The domination of the Pegasus theme in Redon's work is indicative of his feelings about the art of his day. At the time there was a controversy between the artist who let himself be guided by direct observation and the artist who took the memory of observation as his primary guide, between the artist who projected his inner conflicts into everyday reality, and the one who chose for that purpose images taken from mythology or literature. There developed a controversy between the socially concerned and the introvert, generally represented, respectively, by the impressionist and the symbolist—in painting as well as in music and literature. It is quite clear to which trend Redon felt most attracted.

PICASSO, PABLO RUIZ Y

b. Malaga, 1881

Portrait of a Woman—1901

Oil on panel, 52 x 33 cm.

This portrait was probably painted during Picasso's second stay in Paris. One still perceives a certain influence of Toulouse-Lautrec, an influence based more on an affinity of atmosphere than on a style of painting.

In the period from 1890 to 1910, the hat performed numberless functions in Picasso's work; ladies laboriously carried it "like a ship sailing through the greenery," as if signalling with the waving feathers. In the present case there is some uncertainty as to whether the hat makes the wearer more fascinating, more mysterious and charming, or whether it detracts from her unutterable charm because the contrast between her skin and the material of the hat is so great. In the hat and the background Picasso first and foremost relishes the motion of painting and the contrast of the colors and is absorbed in his instrument and his material. In the face, on the other hand, he reaches a curiously still composure because of the absolute concentration of vision, through which he carefully tries to render, in all its nuances, exactly what he sees.

Mrs. Kröller bought this portrait at an auction in 1930—at a time when she had almost stopped making purchases of importance—thus forging a link between the nineteenth and the twentieth centuries.

PICASSO

The Violin—1911-12

Oil on canvas, 100 x 73 cm.

Picasso works the shape elements of a violin into a composition of gray and ochre patches that form various angles to the surface of the picture. In the years 1911-12, Braque and Picasso had reduced their color scheme to the utmost soberness, arriving in consequence at a highly subtle refinement. The problems of form and relief now principally intrigued them. The forms no longer recede into the background, but are directed at the spectator: the space between the picture and the spectator is optically included in the relationship between these two.

An effect similar to that of Van Gogh's work—where roads and fields rush at the spectator like an avalanche—is here arrived at, less emotionally but with a controlled aggressiveness, by putting the planes on the canvas with their sharp edges to the front. The emphatically painted strings and the clearly recognizable violin motifs call up a stimulating tension similar to that of the contrast between the painted and pasted patches in a collage. At this time Braque and Picasso often used an oval canvas, with the nucleus of the picture in the center, so that the vertical-horizontal structure manifests itself more forcibly.

GRIS, JUAN

b. Madrid, 1887–d. Boulogne, 1927

Still Life with Guitar—1915

Oil on canvas, 73 x 92 cm.

In 1906 Juan Gris left his native Spain to move to Paris, where he established himself in the *Bateau Lavoir* ("washerwoman's boat"), the house where Picasso was living too. After having shown nothing but drawings for many years, in 1911 he exhibited a few paintings in which he proved to have applied the cubism of his friends Picasso and Braque in an absolutely personal manner. At the time cubism was in its second, analytical phase, in which the object was divided into an abundance of separately treated little facets. However, in 1915, the year in which this picture was painted, the interest was not so much concentrated on the composition of the elements of form—as it had been in 1911—as on the problem of how, while retaining the objective forms, the foreground, middle plane, and background might be united within the surface of the picture. At times the planes are shifted through each other for this purpose (as in this case the guitar and the palette), at other times the viewpoint is so high that everything (as here the linoleum floor, the table, and the objects on it) is seen in a single plane.

The "fallacious Renaissance perspective" that suggests depth on the flat surface of the canvas is eliminated, and notions of background and foreground are done away with. Gradually the colors and the contours separate themselves from the objects. They are going to lead their own lives, conforming to a rhythm that is no longer determined by the objects, but exclusively by the composition.

GRIS

*Still Life with a Fruit Dish
        and a Water Bottle*—1914

Chalk and oil on linen and paper,
92 x 65 cm.

The cubists continued to introduce innovations; at times they would imitate the grain of wood, marbled paper, and other materials with such deceiving accuracy that they look almost real. Later they went even further, and pasted pieces of paper, chips of wood, and sand onto the canvas, finally heightening these surfaces with crayon or pencil. The traditional axiom that a painting should consist only of oil paint was proved to be just as despotic as the axiom of perspective, and equally determined by the conceptions of a special period.

The cubists showed that the combination of paper and paint is just as convincing in its aesthetic effect as a pure oil painting. Besides—and this is important—the artist, when perspective is no longer considered, develops a keener perception of the depth or relief effect inherent in his colors and materials themselves. All these facets of cubism were realized by Juan Gris, more transparently than by any of the other cubists, by means of a fascinating equilibrium of cylindrical and spherical forms.

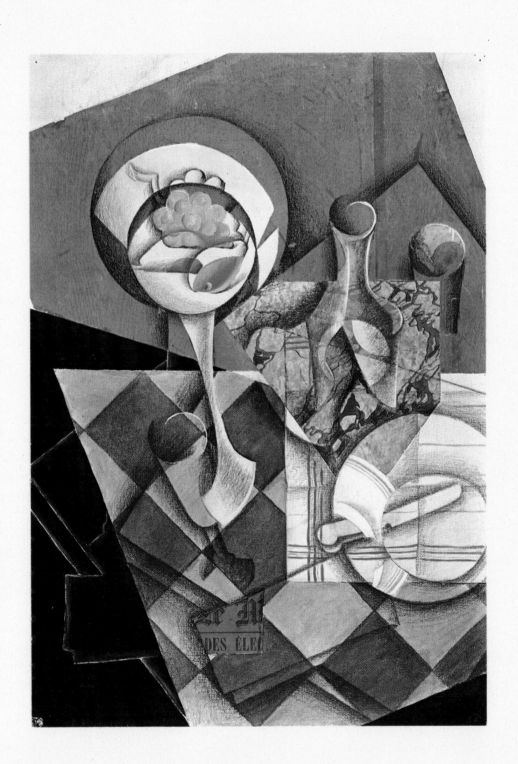

GRIS

Still Life with Syphon—1916

Oil on triplex wood with an oak upper
layer, 73 x 116 cm.

Gris was preeminently a still-life painter. In his work objects
attain a quiet distinction and a solemnity, a presence that human
beings only rarely reach. This insistence on the integrity of objects is supported (and not disrupted, which would seem more
logical) by an artificially intensified shadow effect. Gris's technique here reveals a transitional phase: the effect of light and
shadow is still recognized, but it is used and manipulated by
the artist.

The concrete shapes of things, such as the letters, have not
only an ornamental value, but also the value of a signal: there
arises a tension between object and abstraction, and it is this very
tension that determines the quality of Gris's work. When he
later started working more abstractly and this tension diminished, a sense of vacillation replaced the intensity of his work.
The colors lost their richness, and the contours slackened.

The Kröller-Müller Collection contains fourteen paintings
dating from the period of Gris's purest work (all bought between
1913 and 1927) as well as a series of eight drawings.

BRAQUE, GEORGES

b. Argenteuil, 1882–d. Paris, 1963

Still Life in Diamond Shape, with Guitar—1917

Oil on panel, 60 x 92 cm.

The increasing rigidity which cubism developed after 1914 was manifested in the fact that the oval form disappeared and its function was gradually taken over by the rhomboid. The melting toward the edges, which was so striking in the ovals, appears in this new shape as a shrinking of the planes toward the corners. The accumulated little planes at the right of this painting are kept in balance by the strongly marked angle toward the left of the guitar. It is this balance which gives Braque's work its strictly personal character, together with the fluent touches of the brush in the geometrical forms, and the large planes in a single color which, nevertheless, remain animated because nowhere does the artist conceal or stiffen his handwriting.

The dotted lines seem to imitate the grain of wood, but they are scattered so freely over the surface that they evoke, more than an imitation could do, a decorative staccato effect, an intermezzo between the andante at the left and the presto at the right of the composition.

After 1919-20 we find a turning point in the work of practically all cubist painters, including Braque. Whereas his earlier work had included some large figure pieces, he now turned exclusively to the still life, painting it in a heavier and often more ornamental style than previously.

BRAQUE

Still Life with Playing Cards—1919

Oil on canvas, 50 x 65 cm.

After Braque and Picasso had dissolved their close coopera-
tion of the years 1909 and 1911-12, their works began to show
quite distinct characteristics. Braque used full, quiet colors, including much ochre, olive green, deep brown, and a great deal of
white. His style becomes more painterly (the present picture
suggests the style of painting of a watercolor), the arrangement
is more aesthetic and less daring, and decorative elements play
a more important part. The color of the objects is more essential
than their form.

The predominantly horizontal structure is broken up by the
standing oval of the jug, the playing cards, and the dominoes,
though these latter, in consequence of the ornaments and the
white color that connects them with the surrounding forms, are
actually included in the horizontal movement. Characteristic of
Braque is the equilibrium between the severely tight and the
flowing contours, between the warmer and the cooler colors,
and between the object forms and the geometrical forms.

Mrs. Kröller started to buy Braque's works relatively late
(1920-21). Evidently Gris's work, because of its nobility, cooler
and more aloof than Braque's, struck her more forcibly than the
works of the other cubists. In France itself, however, more attention was paid to Braque's work only after 1922, when he had a
separate room in the *Salon d'Automne.*

LÉGER, FERNAND

b. Argentan, 1881—d. Gif-sur-Yvette, 1955

Soldiers Playing at Cards—1917

Oil on canvas, 129 x 193 cm.

Of Léger's works the Kröller-Müller Museum contains—apart from a series of drawings dating from 1916-21 and two smaller paintings of 1920—his first large cubist canvas (*Nude Figures in a Wood*, painted in 1910), and *Soldiers Playing at Cards*, which was painted after he had been dismissed from active military service in consequence of gas poisoning. Sketches which he had made in the trenches served as his starting point. There is a relationship in color and form with the works that were done immediately before the war, but the colors as well as the forms are more matter-of-fact and rigorous. The new metallic luster is characteristic of this change.

The basic geometrical forms of cubism intensify the ironical, if not sarcastic character of the work: the robot figures, decked out with such human attributes as pipes and medals, await the coming battle and while away the time playing at cards. In this period Léger was harshly confronted with the power of the machine and the relationship of man to machine in all its aspects: man becomes a machine; man productively uses the machine; and—only rarely—man is defenseless before the violence of the machine. After the war it was never possible for Léger to avoid this problem, or to depict it otherwise than very factually and candidly, in very clear colors and uncomplicated, distinctly separated forms.

It seems astonishing that this canvas was bought by Mrs. Kröller so shortly after its completion. In 1921, after she visited Léger's studio together with Henri van de Velde, she wrote: "Nothing in Paris has impressed me so much as his [Léger's] work, although—and this I must honestly confess—during the first five minutes I stood facing it in horror."

140

LÉGER

Mechanical Element—1920

Oil on canvas, 50 x 65 cm.

In 1919 and the following years Léger was quite engrossed in the visual possibilities that the modern city offers the painter. His color is richer than in 1917 and the variations of form have increased. The beauty and utility of the metal things around him enchanted and inspired him. We can easily understand that Henri van de Velde, who likewise felt the vital necessity of entering into a positive relation to The Machine, was deeply impressed by Léger's work. Moreover it is characteristic of the whole collection that Mrs. Kröller, whose mind was on the whole strongly influenced by the spirit of the nineteenth century, so clearly selected this aspect of cubism—its intertwinement with its own time—when assembling works of art.

At the same time this selection indicates how she experienced *Jugendstil:* not as a late offshoot of the nineteenth century, but quite distinctly as a forerunner of the twentieth century that found its confirmation in cubism and in the works of Mondrian and the *de Stijl* group. For these reasons, Léger's work is one of the basic elements of the collection.

MONDRIAN, PIET

b. Amersfoort, 1872–d. New York, 1944

Composition in Line and Color—1913

Oil on canvas, 88 x 115 cm.

By the time Mondrian painted this picture, he had already been living in Paris for a year, and had become acquainted with the work of the cubists, which was just then causing such a tremendous sensation in the annual salon. He wanted, however, to go further than they did—he was seeking to shape an image still further removed from concrete observation. It was not until 1921 that he arrived at a complete dissociation.

More strictly and austerely than in 1912, the division of this canvas into horizontal and vertical principles predominates. The ochre and gray, which in 1911–12 were—for Mondrian, Braque, and Picasso—the two poles from which all intermediate colors derived, are replaced by extremely varied ochre, blue-green, and pinkish lilac. Fundamentally he was already moving in the direction of the primary colors: yellow, blue, and red. The concentration in the center and the mellowing toward the edges is still clearly visible, softening the taut horizontal-vertical scheme. It is as if the contoured patches of color shrink back from touching the frame of the picture, like waves receding from the beach and leaving behind only quivering edges of foam.

Mondrian had not yet reached the water-clear assurance of his work after 1919. Nevertheless, the subtle color sense—the way in which the colors "listen" to each other—as well as the fact that this work is a link between two important periods in Mondrian's development of formal composition, make this picture a highly valuable possession of the museum.

MONDRIAN

Composition in Blue, A—1917

Oil on canvas, 50 x 44 cm.

The so-called plus-minus series came into being between 1914 and 1917 while Mondrian was on the Dutch island of Walcheren. In these images of the pier and the ocean, of the stars, the sky, and the beach, Mondrian had not yet reached what he wanted to achieve: to him this picturing was still too much at random. The leitmotiv of his work in this period is the harmonizing of the imperishable with what is transient and in motion. In the present picture this harmony is realized by the interplay of color and non-color (white). The movement of the colored blocks is defined in their uniting and diverging again as well as in their changes of form. The asymmetry between the left and right halves has become more pronounced.

Mondrian made the acquaintance of the Dutch painter Bart van der Leck in 1916, and a year later, in Leyden, the *de Stijl* group was founded and the magazine of the same name was published. The contact Mondrian had with the artists of the *de Stijl* group (painters, sculptors, and architects) was closer than that with the cubists in Paris. The thinking of this group turned more and more to the function of the work of art in the community, and to the relationship between painting and architecture. And yet Mondrian tore himself free from this group, for he considered any tie with others as an obstacle to his development. In 1919 he returned to Paris.

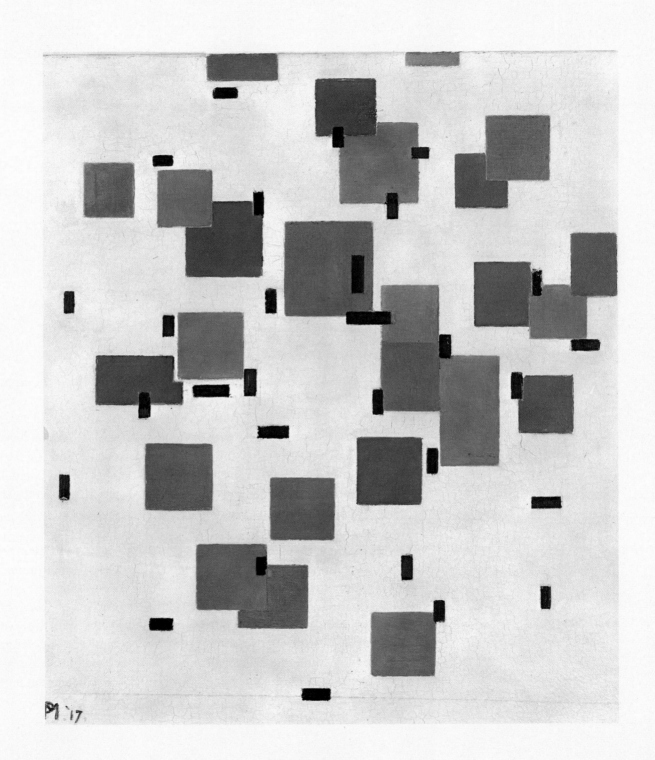

VAN GOGH

Study of a Tree—April 1882

Black crayon, pencil, watercolor, lightly
washed, 49 x 68.5 cm.

Here Van Gogh sets up for the first time with strong emphasis the motif of the bare tree. Although he was to return to this
theme as late as at Auvers, the roots of the tree would never
again be so important a part of the representation. In this drawing the formal relationship between the branches and the roots
is clearly laid down. The network of branches of the vaguely
indicated trees in the background forms a fascinating leftward
countermovement to the heavily drawn foreground branches
with their growth to the right.

The sharp, almost "carved" outlines may well remind one of
the lithograph *Sorrow*, for which Van Gogh drew a preliminary
study in the same month. For Van Gogh there was a direct emotional relationship between the female figure *Sorrow* and this
bare tree: "...Now I tried to put the same sentiment into the
landscape as I put into the figure: the convulsive, passionate
clinging to the earth, and yet being half torn up by the gales. I
wanted to express something of the struggle for life in that pale,
slender woman's figure, as well as in the black, gnarled and
knotty roots...." (Letter 195)

VAN GOGH

Potato Field behind the Dunes—
     July 1883

Brush and ink, heightened with white,
27.5 x 42 cm.

This drawing reveals the watercolor technique in which Vincent worked in the winter of 1882 and the spring of 1883. The white heightenings, which he used to put in relatively sharp accents, are here more integrated in the totality of the image, which has more atmosphere and is more refined than the majority of his drawings. The pattern of the spatial division—the field, bordered by trees, extends straight back, and is fenced off by a horizontal wall—was later used by him repeatedly. The free rhythm of short parallel touches recalls the much later work at Arles, where he filled the surface of his pictures with staccato dots, dashes, and little ornaments.

The close attention paid to the wide landscape predominates here. The busy little figures quite lack their later emphasis and have preeminently an ornamental value: they relieve the zigzag line of the fields of its sharpness, and lengthen the vertical of the trees. The interplay of dark mass and open space is perfectly balanced; this adds to the impression that this drawing came into being in a period of tensionless devotion, unusual with Van Gogh.

VAN GOGH

Reaping Wheat—Summer 1885

Black crayon, heightened with white,
56 x 38 cm.

In the summer of 1885 Van Gogh did a series of about eighty black-crayon studies of peasants at work in the wheat fields, reaping, sheaving, gleaning, and so on. The figures stand large in the picture plane; only rarely is the landscape indicated. The whole attention is concentrated on movement: the motion of the arms, the grip of the hands. The mass of the figures is far more pronounced than in his earlier drawings, where he started primarily from the contour; the black shows nicer nuances in the intermediate tones.

When he started on this series, Vincent wrote to Theo that he intended to make a hundred drawings, if necessary even more. He was fully aware of the fact that he was setting himself a new task for which he would have to develop his technique and his tempo: the peasants had no time for posing, and the crux of the problem was to portray them in their activity without any artificial tensions.

The figures of this series are seen as totalities, the various parts of the body as parts of a living organism with distinct functions. In Van Gogh's letters he constantly refers to the necessity of deformation; he felt that he had to make observation subservient to portrayal.

VAN GOGH

Washerwomen—Early summer 1888

Pen and ink, 31.5 x 24 cm.

Few of Van Gogh's drawings demonstrate so clearly as this one that the rendering of space was one of his essential creative problems. The canal and the adjoining bank are closely connected with each other by means of a dense, straight hatching, and thus isolated from the surrounding pastureland.

The viewpoint is so high that concrete, material representation is completely sacrificed to the ornamental function of the forms. In contrast with many of Van Gogh's paintings, especially those of a later period in which the field in the foreground seems to descend steeply, this drawing leads us to let our eye wander upward from below, so that the grandiose curve finds a resting point in the clearly constructed village in the background.

The problem Van Gogh set himself in Holland in regard to the human figure—that is, how far the artist may go in deforming his observation for the sake of expression—has now been shifted to the landscape. The great firmness of the lines shows that at this time he had full control, intuitively and creatively, over the border between freedom from and adhesion to the object perceived, whereas later, in periods of mental uncertainty, this border often became a problem to be approached as something oppressive and menacing.

BREITNER, GEORGE HENDRIK

b. Rotterdam, 1857–d. Amsterdam, 1923

Foundation Digging (De Bouwput)—
    1897

Pastel, 49 x 43.5 cm.

George Hendrik Breitner was one of the most important painters working in Holland at the turn of the century. For the greater part of his life he worked in Amsterdam, in the midst of the life of the city. The houses along the canals, the horses and the drays, the workmen's wives hastening home late in the afternoon: this is the world from which he took his pictorial motifs.

His open, broad touch and his receptiveness to the anonymous occurrences of city life show a relationship with the impressionists. But in the expressiveness and intensity with which he approached his themes, a tension manifests itself that clearly reveals a simultaneous opposition, whether conscious or unconscious, to impressionism (assuming a definition of an impressionist as a person who passively allows visual impressions to flow in and out of himself). These various elements are represented in *Foundation Digging (De Bouwput):* the impressionistic indication of the color planes, and the grandiose tension in the division of space from a high viewpoint, which gives to the whole an almost dramatic aspect.

REDON

Portrait of Marie Botkine—1900

Pastel, 54 x 48 cm.

Again and again Odilon Redon painted portraits of his wife, his little son, and the wives of his friends—generally in pastel, but occasionally in oil. The female portraits are often represented in a colorful background that is supposed to indicate the mental "atmosphere" of the model. In the portrait of Marie Botkine, however, the background has been utterly suppressed so that the face—quite surrounded by the large hat and the high fur collar, like a pearl in an oyster shell—gets the full emphasis. It seems as if Redon, who in most of his portraits spun around the figure a web of dreamy colors and lines, in this case did not avoid a direct confrontation with his model.

There is a slight irony in the manner in which Marie Botkine carries the hat with the waving feathers. The hairs, the line of the shoulder, and the parallel diagonals of the raised feather, make the little triangle of the face still more conspicuous by their repetition. The same may be said of the subtle contrast between the gray, blue, and black hues on the one hand and the warm reddish brown of the face on the other.

VAN DE VELDE, HENRI

b. Antwerp, 1863–d. Zurich, 1957

Reading Woman—1892-93

Pastel, 47 x 52.5 cm.

Not until 1893 did Van de Velde turn to architecture; until then he was a painter and member of *"Les Vingt,"* the Brussels Artists' Society. The present pastel dates from 1892–93, and is the last of a series of drawings that all portray a woman in an interior.

Here the observed space is turned into an almost sculptural, created space that supports the monumental, heroic portrayal of the woman. The patch of shadow on the floor, especially because of its resemblance in color to the figure, seems to be a tangible presence. The parallel lines possess a great, occasionally aggressive power, and particularly notable is the curiously real little window in this imaginary space.

Even more than his earlier drawings and paintings, this pastel testifies to Van de Velde's leaning towards sculptural architecture. The relationship between the woman and the space, consisting of a formal contrast and a formal resemblance, foreshadows the way in which he will later, for instance, add chimneys to his buildings as individual, almost modeled elements.

PICASSO

Nude Woman—1907-8

Gouache, 62 x 46 cm.

In the years 1906-8, from immediately before to immediately after the painting of his large picture *Les Demoiselles d'Avignon,* Picasso did a series of crayon drawings and gouaches of similar female figures, which show his preoccupation with Negro art, particularly ancient Iberian sculpture, in which at the time French artists were greatly interested.

This drawing reveals the same color, masklike face, and figure built up of contrasting planes that we find in the painting, but the modeling of the bodily forms is much more sculptural than in the painting. From this we may infer that Negro art excited Picasso with the most drastic results only after the painting was for the greater part finished. The almost carved hatchings and the heavily laid on outlines have, notwithstanding the particular character of the gouache, an unprecedented vigor; it is easy to understand why Picasso also made six woodcuts of this figure.

In the years of his blue and pink periods, Picasso was very susceptible to stimulants from the outside world, yet there is nothing groping or unsure in these changing confrontations: he tackles every new formal experiment with the same bold self-confidence and strength of conviction.

GRIS

Still Life—1916

Black crayon, 46.4 x 29.5 cm.

The Kröller-Müller Museum has in its possession eight of Gris's drawings, including some very early ones. The drawings made in 1916 show the full power of Gris's conviction and the masterly command of his craft that had just come to complete maturity. In the rhythmic variation and alternation of flat and convex forms and in the linking together of objective form and geometrical reflection, he realized his ideas with unerring certainty. Without quite relinquishing a relationship to perceived objects, he was concentrating more and more intensively upon the composition of ideal forms, of which the objective forms were only incidental manifestations.

Gris's ultimate goal was not only an aesthetic portrayal, a balancing of shapes and colors; first and foremost he wanted to know whether he could depict "archetypes" on the borderline of their appearance in such natural shapes as bottles, glasses, decanters, and so on. The space of this still life participates in natural as well as created space.

GONZALEZ, JULIO

b. Barcelona, 1876–d. Arceuil, 1942

Self-Portrait—1940

Ink and brush, pencil, 24 x 16 cm.

About ten years ago the Kröller-Müller Museum started assembling a collection of drawings by sculptors to parallel the sculpture collection. In 1955 Mrs. Roberta Gonzalez, on the occasion of the Kröller-Müller's purchase of her father's sculpture, *The Prayer* (1932), presented to the museum a series of six of his drawings. One of these, the self-portrait reproduced here, is not characteristic of a sculptor's drawings, except perhaps for the manner in which the chin, as if made of metal, is put in the face.

But this brush drawing does convey a moving image of the melancholy and loneliness of the artist who, between 1936 and 1950, to commemorate the bombings in his native Spain, produced the Montserrat Sculptures and the *Cactus People*. These works, in their utter despair and defensive gesture, in their intensity and plastic vigor, are comparable to Picasso's *Guernica* (1937). But, where these works have a violent expressiveness unusual in Gonzalez' work, the expression of this *Self-Portrait* is much more introverted, saturated with the sadness of no longer being able to find the words and the images to express his hurt.

MARINI, MARINO

b. Pistoia, 1901

Three Women—probably 1946

Gouache with pastel and ink on paper,
36 x 25 cm.

Marini is one of those artists in whom the creativity of the painter is as great as that of the sculptor. The sculpturally full forms in this pastel drawing clearly suggest the sculptor, and the strong craving for color in the images indicates that in Marini the painter and the sculptor are inseparable.

Toward the end of World War II, Marini had taken refuge in Switzerland. When he returned to Italy in 1946, a new power came into his work: the forms became richer, the colors more intense, the deformations more daring. A comparison with the etching, probably a preliminary study for this pastel drawing, shows to what extent the color, the substance of the crayon, and the rhythm of the parallel undulations of the hip and the abdomen determined the power of the drawing. The motif of Pomona, who appears in Marini's work in various shapes, was as important from 1941 to 1946 as the horseman motif was to be later.

COUZIJN, WESSEL

b. Amsterdam, 1912

Design for a Monument—1951

Colored chalk, 76 x 56 cm.

In 1951 various Dutch sculptors were invited to design a monument for the members of the merchant fleet killed in World War II. When Couzijn concentrated on this task he arrived, among other things, at the present sketch, which gives a clear insight into the character of his work. The principal motif of his work in general is struggle, the release from restraint. Essential is the moment when the mass frees itself, the upward flight representing victory over the down-sucking forces. The opposed forces interlock like wedges. The dramatic way in which the elements—land, water, and sky—are indicated in the background, renders the tension palpable. At the beginning one never knows how the struggle will be decided: the creative forces may win, but so may the destructive; the image may acquire shape, or it may sink into shapelessness.

Had the commission been given to Couzijn, his monument would have been an image not of Death, but of the creative forces that tear themselves away from destruction.

ANONYMOUS: MEXICAN

Colima Valley

Standing Figure—300-600 A.D.

Basalt, height 47 cm.

Mrs. Kröller was aware that sculptures and ceramics from extra-European countries and cultures would not confuse the general impression of her collection, but would enrich it. Quite naturally her attention in the years before World War I was directed toward the East (China, Japan, and Siam) and the ancient (Egyptian, Greek, and Roman). Since 1945, other extra-European plastic forms have come to fascinate the art lover: sculpture from Africa, Oceania, and Mexico—generally works with a magic character. The stimulating influence of this type of sculpture on the cubists and such sculptors as Henry Moore, becomes more apparent when it is shown among a few pieces of high quality; crowding them in a large collection is apt to make for confusion.

The present little statue from the Colima Valley may represent the god of fire, Huehueteotl, who was associated with the volcanic phenomena of that region. Remarkable are the geometric form of the head and the ornamental rendering of the crossed arms.

ANONYMOUS: GREEK

Cypriot Male Figure—ca. 500 B.C.

Limestone, height 46 cm.

The style of the hair and the expression of the face of this figure clearly show the influence of the Greek continent. Mrs. Kröller bought this torso in 1920 at the auction of the collection of Léonce Rosenberg, the Paris art-dealer who was the Maecenas of the French cubists. It is obvious that these circles did not limit themselves to collecting wooden masks from the Congo, as has occasionally been stated with too much emphasis.

About 1920 artists became greatly interested in the torso, which we find, for instance, in the work of Maillol, Arp, Lehmbruck, Duchamp-Villon, Archipenko, Zadkine, and others. They did not consider the torso a mutilated fragment, but rather a strongly concentrated plastic form, whose intensity and expressivity are so overpowering that arms and legs cannot affect the final impression. It is a center of energy which, by its very limitation, appeals more strongly to the imagination of the spectator than the whole body could do.

ANONYMOUS: CHINESE

T'ang Dynasty

Horse (Mortuary Figure)—618-906 A.D.

Earthenware, height 54 cm.

Small Chinese mortuary figures (horses, camels, priests, dancing girls, and so on), especially at the beginning of the eighth century, possess a great purity and monumentality. In consequence of the tension in the head and the legs, the plastic vigor of the hindquarters, and the mat tints of the decayed glazing, this horse has a grandeur and an exquisite grace that are often lacking in the mortuary figurines of later periods. It is quite understandable that a sensitive sculptor like Marini was particularly struck by this combination of fervency and silent submission.

The contiguity within the collection of the ancient Chinese *Horse* to the big wooden *Horse and Rider* by Marini brings us closer to the dream of the *Musée Imaginaire*, whose content is independent of time and country. It is the dream of every collector who will not allow himself to be deluded by the song of the academic sirens.

ANONYMOUS: FLEMISH

Mechlin

Madonna Standing on Half-Moon—
1520-30

Polychromed walnut, height 41 cm.

From the middle of the fifteenth century the Immaculate Conception of the Virgin is expressed by the figure of Mary standing on a half-moon. (In the *Laudes Marianae* Mary is described "as beautiful as the moon," and the Apocalyptic Madonna is also pictured as standing on a crescent.) The Mechlin Madonnas, who generally have unloosened, long hair and occasionally wear a little ribbed cap, usually have a wide, curved forehead, heavy eyelids, and a preciously diminutive mouth and nose.

In the present example the Child has a quite individual personality, and is sitting upright on the arm of the Madonna, free from her figure. The Madonna stands erect in her bell-shaped dress, her belly and left hip slightly curved. The flat back shows the extent to which these images are conceived in relation to architectural elements.

The Kröller-Müller Collection possesses only a small group of sculpture from the late Middle Ages but, together with the pictures painted at that time, they evoke in a concise but unmistakably clear way the modeling typical of that period.

RODIN, AUGUSTE

b. Paris, 1840—d. Meudon, 1917

Crouching Woman (La Luxure)—1882
Bronze, height 95 cm.

This figure was intended as part of the preliminary model for the *Gate of Hell* and we see it, in a somewhat modified shape, to the right of *The Thinker*. The *Gate of Hell* was meant for the Museum of Decorative Arts in Paris. Rodin worked at it from 1880 to 1888, but the project acquired such forms that the government rescinded the commission. The original instructions called for "a decorative door representing an ensemble of bas-reliefs drawn from Dante's *Divina Commedia*."

Rodin, who was a great admirer of Dante's, at first limited himself to *Inferno*, but he later became so deeply engrossed in his task that he exceeded all the limits of his theme, and made the *Gate of Hell* a manifestation of all imaginable forms of human tragedy. The forms too became more and more emotional of action; the figures wrenched themselves free from the sleekness of the surface and the pathos of their gestures ignored all architectonic limitations.

The *Crouching Woman*, strongly related to Michelangelo's *Squatting Boy*, reveals all the characteristics of Rodin's work of this period: the emotional tension, the mobile surface, and the perfect domination over the sculptural mass. The work, by means of the tilting of the head and the position of the arms and legs pressed against the body, acquires a clenched compactness full of explosive force.

ROSSO, MEDARDO

b. Turin, 1858–d. Milan, 1928

Child in the Sun—1892

Wax, height 34.5 cm.

Rosso is a sculptor who has only recently been taken notice of. Etha Fles, whom he met in Holland in 1900, devoted herself until her death in 1948 to making the public familiar with his work. Boccioni was among the artists interested in Rosso's work: Rosso went so far in scanning and rendering visible the effects of light as to bring the time problem of the futurists within the confines of consciousness.

The little planes of light and shade are so tiny, and they merge so imperceptibly, that we feel inclined to scan the surface ourselves, to walk round Rosso's sculptures in order to follow the curves. He preferred to work in wax because this material is so susceptible to the slightest touch of the fingers. He chose as models children and sick or elderly people whose faces were not deeply wrinkled, whose features were either blurred or undeveloped.

The borderline between sculpture and surroundings fades to a great extent; the sculptor often lets the visible shape emerge from the unfashioned material by causing the latter to envelop the image like an amorphous mass.

LEHMBRUCK, WILHELM

b. Duisburg Meiderich, 1881–
d. Berlin, 1919

Female Nude—1910

Baked concrete, height 193 cm.

From 1910 to 1914 Lehmbruck worked in Paris. His special admiration was directed toward Rodin and Maillol, but at the same time he had personal contacts with Brancusi, Modigliani, and Archipenko. In Paris he freed himself from all academic frigidity, and his sculptures of 1910-11 have more opulent and flowing forms than ever before or afterward. The present sculpture has, nevertheless, a certain unapproachableness, an introverted melancholy. Maillol's influence, mentioned so often, was quite absorbed by Lehmbruck and converted into a plastic form which, however, lacks Maillol's candor and vitality.

After 1912 Lehmbruck's craving for stylization increased, his figures became more elongated, the forms more angular, the structure more austere. In the curved figures the relationship of the almost linear mass to the open space became more and more important. A tension begins to manifest itself in his work, and perhaps a lack of confidence in his own power as well—which, in 1910 when he modeled the *Female Nude,* was as yet quite latent.

BOURDELLE, EMILE-ANTOINE

b. Montauban, 1861–d. Le Vésinet, 1929

The Large Penelope—1912

Bronze, height 240 cm.

On the large lawn of the sculpture park of the Kröller-Müller Museum stands Bourdelle's *Penelope,* straight and sturdy of shape like a tree. The head, slightly inclined to the left and supported by the triangle of the arms, is kept aloft by the curved mass of the body. The expression of the face and the shape of the head free the statue of any allusion to a Germanic world. One does not think of the Norns but of the Furies, awaiting and yet dominating the outcome of events.

Bourdelle knew perfectly how to convey a Greek monumentality. He deeply admired the ancient Greeks and often took his themes from their mythology; even his modeling has occasionally something archaistic about it. This predilection is never rational or academic, but is rather part of the life in the South of France to which Bourdelle was innately attached, even while he was living in Paris. His female figures, even his Madonnas, belong in a Greek temple built on the rocks, facing the open sea on one side and a wide fertile plain on the other. The space within a church would be too cramped for them, and the architecture too domineering.

Bourdelle made several preliminary studies for *Penelope* in the years from 1905 to 1912, all of them smaller in size.

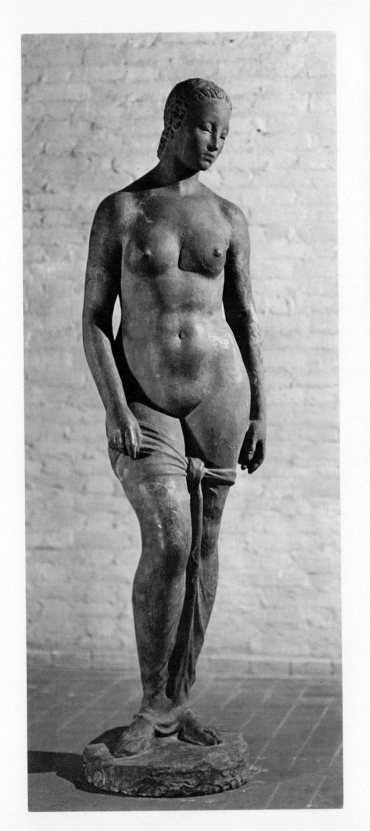

MAILLOL, ARISTIDE

b. Banyuls-sur-mer, 1861–
d. Marly-le-Roy, 1944

The Air—1938-39

Lead, 140 x 255 cm.

This sculpture was commissioned by the city of Toulouse in memory of the aviators killed in service. The original version, in stone, did not entirely satisfy Maillol, and he continued working on a version in plaster of Paris with the intention of making a lead cast of it later (this was only done in 1962 at the request of the Kröller-Müller Foundation). The stone version rests in a shell-shaped drapery, and is closely related to Maillol's monument for Cézanne (dating from 1921–25). By leaving out the drapery and by slightly tilting the body, Maillol has strengthened the expressiveness of the lead version: it has become clearer that it is floating, and the almost commanding gesture with which the clouds are pushed away is more pronounced. Even the color of the lead serves to intensify the expression.

The structure, determined by the powerful verticals of the neck and the right arm in opposition to the stretched left arm and the legs, is perfectly integrated in the representation, as is always the case with Maillol. All stiffness is excluded by the flowing curve from the head to the right leg. It is to this clarity of structure that this sculpture owes its almost divine power, comparable only with Bourdelle's *Penelope* and Maillol's own *The River* (dating from 1939–43). *The Air* sprang from a world where everything has its own perfectly distinct and unassailable function.

ARP, JEAN

b. Strasbourg, 1887

Cloud Herdsman—1953
Bronze, height 167 cm.

Perhaps the atmosphere of Arp's work has been best expressed by himself in his often repeated definition: "Art is a fruit that grows in man as a fruit grows on a plant or the child in its mother's womb." Inseparable from his plastic work are Arp's poems; quite rightly Marchiori, describing *Cloud Herdsman,* refers to Arp's *"Taches dans le vide"* (Spots in the Void): "The end of the air and the end of the world are round like balloons." In this borderland between heaven and earth, the majority of Arp's images come into existence, swelling out of the earth like fruits or flitting down from the sky like big drops or dead leaves, in a movement that has neither beginning nor end, at times extremely sensual but never soft.

Having begun as a contributor to and a leader of the dadaist Cabaret Voltaire in Zurich, Arp very soon took his own line. Like the others, he let himself be guided by his own sense of form, but he was never so provocative in his creations. From the beginning his free sculptures and reliefs have had a strong relationship with nature, without being an imitation of nature. In consequence of their compact and very pure authenticity, they form a world entirely their own. Arp's work is best defined by his own words: *"constructions végétatives."*

186

DUCHAMP-VILLON, RAYMOND

b. Damville, 1878–d. Cannes, 1918

Head of Baudelaire—1911

Bronze, height 40 cm.

Raymond Duchamp-Villon—brother of the painters Marcel Duchamp, Jacques Villon, and Suzanne Duchamp—began sculpting when he had to interrupt his medical studies during a period of convalescence. His contacts with the futurists clearly permeate a part of his work, and his longing for pure structure brought him into touch with architecture (at the 1912 Salon d'Automne he exhibited the plan for a cubistic house, planned with André Maré).

The Head of Baudelaire is one of Duchamp-Villon's earliest works. It does not yet show the typically cubist deformations influenced by African art, but the high dome of the skull, the flattening of the temples and ears, and the heavy column of the neck clearly indicate the desire to penetrate into the essential of form. As a result of the austere construction, the powerful nose, and the mordantly demoniac mouth, this Baudelaire has acquired a presence utterly different from that of the little etching by Manet or the portrait by Courbet. These latter images did express Baudelaire's dandy-like and poetic qualities but did not stress the diabolically charming character of his art.

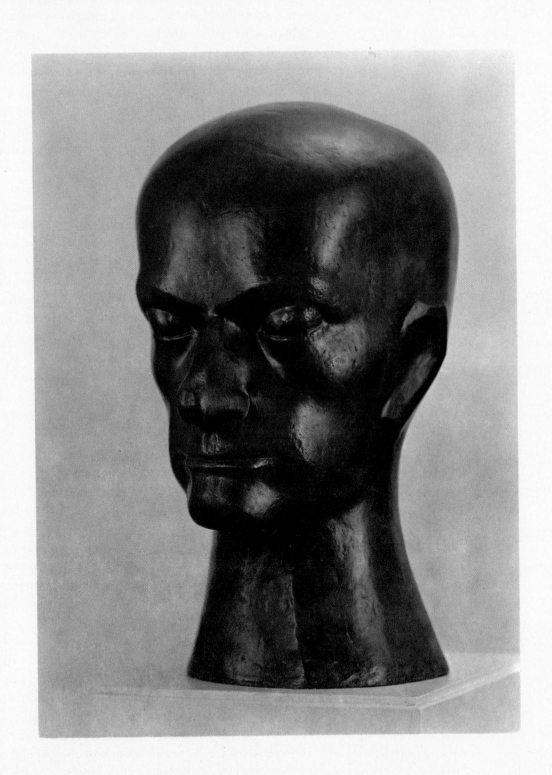

ZADKINE, OSSIP

b. Smolensk, 1890

Torso Clementius—1941

Veined marble, height 98 cm.

During World War II Zadkine emigrated to the United States. Out of a marble sepulchral column found on the 1893 grave of a Negro named John Clement, Zadkine carved this torso. The structure of the column was maintained as much as possible, and it is precisely from the original angularity—prominent, for instance, in the legs—that the sculpture derives its convincing power and intensity. The engraved hand, admitting of several interpretations, acts like a poetic addition; considering the frequency with which the same device occurs in Zadkine's work, it must undoubtedly be highly important to him.

Zadkine's torsos entirely lack the baroque polymorphous element of his other works. A certain ambiguity may occur, but the manner in which the ambivalent expressions present themselves avoids the multiform excesses that render some of his works hard to decipher. In *Torso Clementius* he arrived at a splendid synthesis between the hard material and his own craving for polished forms, between angular planes and slight curves.

LIPCHITZ, JACQUES

b. Druskieniki, 1891

Song of the Vowels—1930-31

Bronze, height 200 cm. (without base)

About 1926, after a cubistic period in which Lipchitz' forms stiffened, the relationship of mass to space became essential to his sculpture. In the beginning we find "transparents" in which the mass is reduced almost to a linearly undulating pattern; after that form becomes fuller and the tension between mass and space increases. The relationship between the human figure and the musical instrument, which had fascinated the cubists (Juan Gris was an intimate friend of Lipchitz), has acquired in *The Song of the Vowels* a significance that far exceeds formal considerations. Here a metamorphosis is taking place, whose final phase has not been reached: force and counterforce are so strong as to equilibrate each other in the struggle—or the embrace. This image fixes a moment of violent tension, which finds neither a solution nor a discharge.

And this happens not only in the present sculpture, but also in the majority of Lipchitz' works. The miracle is that the forces, tending toward each other, are subjected to the will of the sculptor, are shaped by him. The creative force evokes a tension without leading to an explosion of form; in Lipchitz' works of this period space and mass are absolutely equivalent. The flowing vehemence of the forms is checked by the angular planes. Their profusion is subjected to a clear discipline.

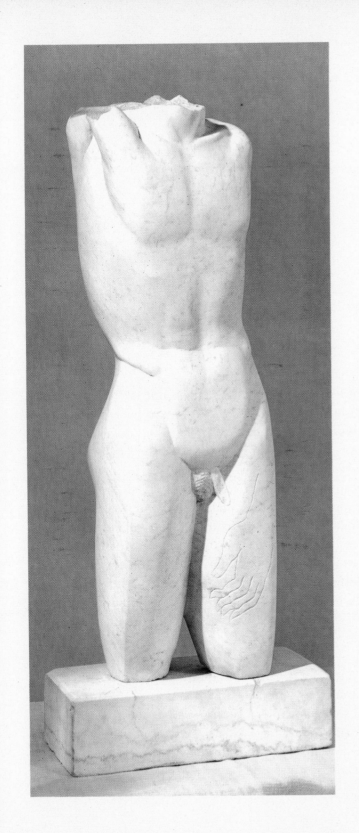

MARINI

Horse and Rider—1951-55

Painted wood, height 212 cm.

The motif of horse-and-horseman is one of the principal themes in Marini's work. As early as 1935 he made a large equestrian sculpture in wood, and in the ensuing years—with a culminating period between 1945 and 1951—he again and again took up the same subject, in wood and in bronze, often colored. In the beginning there was a marked affinity to Etruscan and Roman sculpture. The simple daily observation of horses and riders (he had rented his studio from the owners of a riding academy) fascinated him to such an extent that the longing for an emotional identification did not yet arise. In the early work there is a perfect balance of energy between the horseman and the horse; in both of them an alert concentration dominates.

But after World War II—when Marini had seen herds of desperate horses, deserted by their masters, rushing wildly through the Po Valley—the intuitively felt unity of man and animal is weakened. The rider is scared, enraptured, or amazed; the horse stretches, strains its muscles, and becomes more angular in shape. Planes of color intensify the atmosphere of apocalyptic panic. Later still the horse rears backward, almost throwing the rider, and the triangles of color begin to lead a perfectly independent—nearly abstract—life.

HEPWORTH, BARBARA

b. Wakefield, 1903

Curved Form with Inner Form: Anima
—1959

Bronze, diameter 169 cm., inner form 52 cm.

Few works of art so completely evoke the landscape in which they took shape as do Barbara Hepworth's sculptures. This does not mean that the forms of the waves, the rocks, or the plants at St. Ives, Cornwall, are to be found in her work; but the force that drives the waves, shapes the rocks, and nourishes the plants, is felt in the forms of her sculpture. In contrast with many young sculptors, she does not allow herself to be influenced by the accidental nature of her material, but rather solidifies, with the utmost purity, the construction she considers essential to her conception. To quote her own words: "you must take every idea to its ultimate conclusion with all the sincerity and passion of which one is capable."

This absolutism is characteristic of all of Hepworth's work. Each sculpture gives the impression of a pure perfection which, like ripe fruit, still holds the possibility of a new fruitfulness. These works, in which the outward movement turns inward again, do not give the impression of aloofness—certainly never of repellent harshness. In *Anima* the "curved form" receives the "inner form," but does not hold it imprisoned; the "inner form" is supported by the "curved form," but is not attached to it. The fact is, rather, that the boring through the material—the piercing toward the nucleus which was long essential to Hepworth— gives the spectator the impression that the nucleus of the sculpture block is unfolding from within. The heart is not taken away, but space makes its way from within, through the mass of matter, in slow convolutions.

MOORE, HENRY

b. Castleford, 1898

Reclining Figure II—1960

Bronze, 129.5 x 259 cm.

One of the chief motifs in Moore's work is the reclining female figure. This theme has occurred in his work since 1929. The first works are in stone and show the influence of the works of Mexican art he had seen in the British Museum. The later works, in bronze, become more and more "landscape-like," giving the impression of mighty rocky formations.

In 1959 the figure appeared for the first time in two parts: the torso with a small head is separate from the enormous bridge of the legs. But even this form was anticipated at a much earlier date, in the geometrical forms of 1933–34, in which there is a distinct relationship between the high shape, curving to the front, and the flat, round shape underneath. The openings within the parts, and the space between the parts, are changeable in character: at times the gap is a sloping valley surrounded by the protecting walls of the body; at other times it is a funnel, or a more aggressively hewn-out hole.

Reclining Figure II owes its tension to the ambivalent quality of the violent breaking up into two parts, and the groping toward each other of the *"disjecta membra."* The surface is treated elaborately, occasionally almost plowed over. The image is ancient yet timeless; a prehistorical symbiosis is brought about between man and animal. The upward movement of the half-raised torso finds a descending fulfillment in the legs, as sturdy as old trees. The horizontal sections in between are full of grooved rises and hollows. This sculpture seems to have been modeled not only by the wind but also by the water.

196

WOTRUBA, FRITZ

b. Vienna, 1907

Relief—1960

Marble, 210 x 75 cm.

Wotruba displays in his work an almost brusque concentration upon the fundamental structure of the standing, sitting, or reclining human being—particularly the standing man, alone or in a row of two, three, or more. Yet his work is never the sterile result of an obsession: due to the keen nuances of his feeling for his material—be it stone, bronze, or marble—each sculpture has its own individuality and is a separate solution of the problem. Wotruba's preference for a rough type of stone with a granulated surface renders his works less inaccessible and less aloof than they might be in some polished material. When two or more figures stand side by side, as in *Relief,* a very lively relationship is brought about as the result of slight variations and shiftings.

During World War II Wotruba took refuge in Switzerland. When he returned to Vienna in 1945, and was appointed to a professorship at the academy of arts, the transition from prosperous Switzerland to partly destroyed Vienna came as a terrible shock. Nevertheless, the beauty of the ruins acted as a charm. But, as Wotruba himself said: "It is not my business to give to perishable things more importance than they have received already in literature, drama, and the film. What is important to me is the figure, the sculpture, the statics, the proportion, the balance, and finally the unity."

ARMITAGE, KENNETH

b. Leeds, 1916

Monitor—1961

Bronze, 152.5 x 198 cm.

In 1960 Armitage was commissioned to make a sculpture for the principal facade of Chateau Mouton Rothschild near Bordeaux. This sculpture, which was to have some relation to the Rothschild vineyards, occupied Armitage's mind so intensely, and fascinated him so deeply, that all thoughts and images thus roused remained active in his work for many years afterward. For the commission he made an irregular oval relief—a sun—with a clean-cut and pronounced head personifying divine power. But while he was working, there emerged more and more often, and every time more intensely, the memory of the fungi he had once found growing in horizontal layers on a moldering tree trunk. This memory too was incorporated into the image, which he justified in the following way: "the parallel lines would echo the regimented lines of vines that extend as far as the eye can see; they might be faintly reminiscent of organic and rudimentary limbs springing from the belly of the sun."

This evolution of one of Armitage's images shows clearly that it is seldom possible to attribute a single, distinctly recognizable motif to any image. While the artist works, innumerable visions are remembered which will contribute to the determination of the image and the whole further development of the artist's work. Armitage has always been fascinated by the relationship between horizontal and vertical, and by the tension brought about among human beings moving in an open space. In *Monitor* and other sculptures, all this is united in the relationship of the protruding limbs to each other and to the large flat surface, as well as in the relationship of these limbs to the linear pattern engraved in the surface. In comparison with Armitage's earlier work, we find here a distinct increase in plastic power.

200

PAN, MARTA

b. Budapest, 1923

Floating Sculpture "Otterlo"
—1960-61

Plastic, 180 x 226 cm.

Two works were especially commissioned for the first lawn of the Sculpture Park of the Kröller-Müller Museum: a large, austere granite sculpture by Hans Aeschbacher—which forms a relationship between the severe architecture of the museum building and the park—and the present sculpture by Marta Pan. Together with her husband, the architect André Wogenscky, she also designed the pond in which her sculpture floats and the path around it.

It was clear that the park should contain a pond, so that the wind would not only stir the vertically growing treetops but also ripple the horizontal surface of the water. It was therefore decided that there ought to be a feather-light sculpture in the pond that would represent the movement of nature. Best suited to undertake this project was Marta Pan who, since her arrival in Paris in 1947, had continually occupied herself with the relationship between sculpture and landscape, and with the vital reality of equilibrium. Only after years of calculation and experiment was the form—which had first been made in wood—cast by the St. Gobain Workshop. The upper section, the "hat," is fixed upon a little ball on top of the floating lower section, and reacts to the slightest breath of wind. The lower section is stabilized internally by means of lead, and moves independently of the upper section.

This sculpture is no mere imitation of a swan or any other water bird. Its harmony—more absolute than any found in the world of nature, and more beautiful and richer than any found in the world of dreams—is the plastic harmony of the concave and the convex, of the hollow and the sphere, of open and closed forms, of keenly accentuated forms reaching out for but not touching each other, of the round curve and the long flowing line. It is also the harmony of the pure white, smooth material and the rugged surface of water, grass, and trees.

KEMENY, ZOLTAN

b. Banica, Transylvania, 1907

Involuntary Velocity—1962

Brass, 100 x 100 cm.

Zoltan Kemeny works exclusively on reliefs of prefabricated metal elements (nails, screws, tubes, etc.), or of strips of metal which he cuts, bends, and welds. To him a relief represents "color in motion"; "the differences in level in the work indicate the various levels of the color in motion:—the distance between the back wall and the various layers of colors could vary from a millimeter to a meter." This sensitivity to color, which Kemeny varies by soldering or welding, or by use of different metals, is essential. It is a sensitivity intimately connected with the lyricism of the titles he gives to his works. Because of the rhythm of his reliefs, the movement of the metal elements, his work almost seems to be materialized music. As a result of this melodious character his work stands apart from other scrap-metal sculpture that utilizes the beauty and vitality of corroded and dilapidated matter; to Kemeny it is basically unimportant whether such elements as screws have been used or have come straight from the factory, and he remodels, recolors, and organizes them into compositions that recognize and confirm the vital value of beauty.

Involuntary Velocity is one of Kemeny's most powerful and concentrated reliefs. The austerity of the small angular blocks of brass of varying height, the interlocking double circular movement that seems to continue beyond the surface, and the strong contrast between the shining spots and shaded stretches give the relief a virile force and a firmness. These factors make us conscious of the prototypically elementary character of the spiral movement not as a manneristic or baroque labyrinth but as an original architectural form.

ZOLTAN NEMENY GEB. 1907
GRWELLENSURGE (MELLIKG) 1962

MÜLLER, ROBERT

b. Zurich, 1920

The Heart—1963

Iron, 165 x 100 cm.

Müller's sculptures are generally constructed of iron parts, curved or angular, pointed or flat, voluminous or threadlike. His is a world full of warring elements and complications which are, however, so energetically arranged that confusion is definitely excluded. There is often strife in the fierce confrontation of full, round, or murderously pointed elements. At times Müller's sculptures are standing directly on the floor; at other times, as in the case of *The Heart*, the "pedestal" is part of the image and is made of the same metal.

Müller's recent work, especially that of the last two years, has a masterly—perhaps magical—power of conviction. The construction is simpler and the forms are larger; there is less picturing here, but more is suggested with an intense enchantment. The movement is no longer so complicated and whirling, but the shapes embrace each other and cling together.

The memory of the heap of scrap metal in which Müller had himself photographed many years ago has faded, as has the memory of his *"objets trouvés."* The pieces of metal are so intensely labored by him and correspond to his vision so completely that the accidental, the mental flash is no longer recognized. As is the case with every strong vision, his work is more convincing by its continuity than because of a surprising or whimsical mental impulse.